Love Handles
for the
Romantically Impaired

Books by Laura Jensen Walker

Dated Jekyll, Married Hyde
Love Handles for the Romantically Impaired
Mentalpause
Thanks for the Mammogram!
Through the Rocky Road and into the Rainbow Sherbet

Love Handles

for the

Romantically Impaired

Laura Jensen Walker

SPIRE

© 1998 by Laura Jensen Walker

Published by Fleming H. Revell
a division of Baker Book House Company
P.O. Box 6287, Grand Rapids, MI 49516-6287
www.bakerbooks.com

Spire edition published 2003

Previously published by Bethany House Publishers

Printed in the United States of America

0-8007-8711-0

Unless otherwise indicated, Scripture is taken from the HOLY BIBLE, NEW INTERNATIONAL VERSION®. NIV®. Copyright © 1973, 1978, 1984 by International Bible Society. Used by permission of Zondervan. All rights reserved.

Scripture marked KJV is taken from the King James Version of the Bible.

For Lisa,
my sister, my friend,
fellow writer and book lover,
with love

Laura Jensen Walker is the author of several humor books, including *Dated Jekyll, Married Hyde; Thanks for the Mammogram!; Mentalpause;* and *Through the Rocky Road and into the Rainbow Sherbet*. A popular speaker and breast cancer survivor, she knows firsthand the healing power of laughter. She and her husband, Michael, have a laughter-filled home in Northern California, which they share with their piano-playing dog.

Acknowledgments

Deepest gratitude, first of all, to God for His gifts and for making my dreams come true. Additionally, this book couldn't have been written without the help and support of the following people:

To my wonderful husband, Michael: You are the love handle I hold on to. Thanks for your sacrificial love and for hanging in there through all those "starving writer" months (years)—and lots of budget microwave meals. Thanks also for giving me that much-needed male perspective! *Je t'adore.*

To my parents, Mort and Bettie Eichenberg: Thank you for always believing in me. And to my father, David C. Jensen: Thanks for passing on that "dream gene," Dad. I miss you.

To Katie Young, whose sense of humor and unflagging enthusiasm for this project was always such a boost—thanks for reading all those first and second drafts! (And for honestly telling me on occasion, "This part's not so funny," thereby challenging me to be even better.)

To Lana Yarbrough: Who daily exemplifies what it means to be a "best friend." I love you. To Steve and Chris and the rest of the Pond family: Thanks for letting me camp out at your lovely home with a view while I picked your brains for chapter input.

To Roger Keskeys: Thanks for being the best singles pastor ever. It was a privilege serving with you.

To Todd Michero and the Wednesday Night Singles Group at Fair Oaks Presbyterian Church: Thanks for letting me use you as "guinea pigs"!

To Brad Sargent: Thanks for the chapter title *"You're How Old, and You Still Live With Your Mother?"* (Thanks, too, to the rest of Al Janssen's Mount Hermon brainstorming group.)

To Barb Peil: Thanks for that last-minute tinkering at Mount Hermon. You're a doll!

To Elisabeth Brown Hendricks, who wrote me that her boyfriend was "romantically impaired": I'm happy to hear he got over his impairment long enough to propose! Many blessing on your marriage, and thanks for one half of a great book title!

To my editor—and friend, Steve Laube: Thank you, more than I can say, for making the whole writing/editing experience such a pleasure (even with your Vlad-the-Impaler red pen).

Finally, to all my friends and family who cheered me on and allowed me to tell their stories: Thank you, more than I can say, for your encouragement (and great anecdotes). And to everyone else who filled out surveys or shared their "romantically impaired" tales: Thanks for lots of laughs!

Contents

Introduction

Years ago, as a starry-eyed single Christian woman, I longed to be swept off my feet by some tall, handsome, godly man who would propose sweetly to me on bended knee with a look of rapt adoration in his eyes (in some wildly romantic setting, of course). Well, God sent me a very handsome, godly man—just half an inch taller than me. And he proposed . . . in his car—which kind of eliminates the bended-knee part—(although he did have that look of rapt adoration I yearned for).

Not exactly the incredibly romantic situation I'd envisioned. However, I didn't let that stop me from recognizing true love when I saw it, so I grabbed it.

We all have romantic expectations (*occasionally* unrealistic) about the person we love—whether we're single or married, male or female. And we can become frustrated or disappointed when our mate (or potential mate) doesn't live up to those expectations.

To that I say . . . "Lighten up! Cut 'em some slack!"

Although I'm saying that to myself too. My husband—an incredibly romantic guy when we were dating and for the first couple years of our marriage—has a tendency to be a little romantically impaired every now and then.

But then again, so do I.

I'm not always in the mood to be romantic—sometimes my idea of romance is a good book and a bubble bath—but that doesn't mean I want to throw out the romance with the bath water.

One thing I know for sure: even when I may not be "in the mood," I plan to hang on to love for dear life.

In the process, I wanted to share a few "love handles" with you so that when the one you love acts a little romantically impaired, you'll know you're not alone. (And if all else fails, you can always just grab 'em in a great big lip lock!)

1

Wooings, Weddings, and PMS Proposals

Off-the-wall wooings and quirky proposals.

THEIR ROMANCE BEGAN with a nosebleed.

Warren had noticed Diane around the U.S. Air Force base in Germany where they were both stationed, and had even talked to her a few times.

He was definitely interested.

But she was engaged and, therefore, off limits.

The engagement ended, however, and shortly thereafter Diane started getting nosebleeds.

Seeking help for her condition, she whisked into the base's Ear, Nose, and Throat clinic.

And ran into Warren. Who worked there as a medical technician.

The first treatment the doctor tried to stop the bleeding didn't work, so Diane had to come back again—fortuitously. This time they had to cauterize the blood vessels inside her nose—using an electric current.

"Warren's hanging on to the box that runs the electrical current—adjusting the knobs; the doctor's sticking things up my nose; and I'm gripping the handrails of my chair with tears running down my face," Diane recalls.

But painful as the procedure was, it worked. Diane's nosebleeds stopped.

And Warren started. Falling in love, that is.

Was it love at first volt?

However, it wasn't until two months later, when Diane had to come in for a tonsillectomy, that things really started happening.

Already falling for Diane in a big way, Warren didn't have the heart to assist in her surgery. However, as soon as she was in recovery, he made his move.

Every night for the entire week she was hospitalized,

Warren would come to visit—bearing cards, flowers, even teddy bears.

"He'd just sit there and talk and talk and talk," says Diane. "The nurses couldn't really kick him out because he was hospital personnel." (If the women in white said anything to Warren, he'd just answer, "I'm here for her recovery.")

Part of that recovery meant Diane had to wear an olive-drab sling packed with ice under her chin and tied on top of her head. The rest of her stunning ensemble included a hospital gown, greasy hair, and glasses. (With the sling tied to her head, she couldn't wash her hair, and the hospital insisted she wear glasses rather than her contacts.)

Still Warren kept coming back—night after night—with gifts.

"I thought, *If this guy cares for me seeing me at my worst, then it must be someone special,*" Diane says.

That's when *she* began to fall—in love, that is.

The day she was discharged from the hospital, she and Warren had their first official date.

Less than two months later, he proposed. And two and a half months after that, they were married.

They've lived happily-ever-after ever since—without one nosebleed.

My first meeting with Michael (now my husband) wasn't quite so dramatic.

We met at a singles retreat after I'd walked away from the Lord for a while.

I was angry at God for not bringing me a mate—after years of waiting—and I'd hardened my heart against Him in hurt rebellion. But now I was at the place where I was taking tentative steps back to Christ, and my best friend, Lana, thought the retreat would be a good place to begin.

Great. Another singles retreat, I thought cynically. *A great place to reaffirm my undesirability.*

But I went. Albeit reluctantly.

The first night there was a talent show and some guy sang "Joseph's Song" by Michael Card. But this guy didn't just *sing* it. He *became* Joseph—Jesus' earthly father.

As I listened to the words through this man's dramatic interpretation, the hard protective shell I'd allowed to grow around my heart cracked and all the bitter pieces fell away—leaving me weeping.

That singer was Michael.

We were married nine months later.

But he doesn't even remember meeting me at the retreat!

What he does remember is first hearing about me at a men's retreat two months later.

My friend Steve was assigned to the same room as Michael, and after finding out that he loved music, movies, and the theater, he told him he had a friend Michael "just had to meet."

That friend was me.

Steve was a little slow in setting us up, however. By the time he finally arranged for us to meet, Michael and I had already been on three dates.

From the beginning, we just clicked. (For me, it was love at first note.)

We saw a lot of each other in a very short period of time and things started to get serious pretty quickly. However, once I saw the direction our relationship was heading, I knew there was something very difficult I needed to do: get tested for AIDS.

Although I'd been celibate a long time, I knew that I was at risk due to my past.

So I told Michael—who'd been a Christian since elementary school—that I was going to get tested, and if by chance I had AIDS, that would be the end of our relationship.

"No, it won't," Michael said matter-of-factly.

"What?" I asked in astonishment.

He took my hand, held it tightly, looked deep into my

eyes and said, "Laura, I love you. If you're sick, we'll adjust. It will complicate things, but we'll make it work."

The test came back negative, but I was positive.

Positively in love.

A scant six weeks after our first date, Michael popped the question.

He hadn't planned on asking me quite that early, however. In fact, he was working out an intricate, romantic proposal a little further down the line.

But my raging PMS attack thwarted his plans.

One of our favorite romantic movies is *Somewhere in Time* with Christopher Reeve and Jane Seymour. And there's one scene in the movie where the bereaved couple think they've lost each other forever when, suddenly, Jane spots Christopher (Richard) from a distance.

"Richard!" she screams, running toward him with open arms.

At this critical juncture in the movie, Michael was planning to have one of his techno-video pals splice in a film clip of him—running toward me saying, "Laura . . . will you marry me?"

But I blew it. Thanks to PMS. (Proposal Mess-up Syndrome.)

I don't remember exactly what started my hormonal attack that night, but I do know that I was crying and carrying on about our relationship and saying that maybe we should just break it off. I felt awful and was bent on proving it.

In the midst of my blubbering, Michael asked me to marry him.

No fool was I.

If this guy could propose after seeing me at my worst, he was definitely a keeper.

Then there was the couple brought together by a drunken dog.

Andrea found a sick dog stumbling and retching on

the street behind her house, so she took it inside to care for it.

However, the poor puppy kept throwing up, and Andrea didn't know what to do.

Concerned, she called her friend Bill for help—who hurried right over.

Bill took one look at the sick puppy and said, "This dog's drunk . . . and he's a pit bull."

Andrea nursed the dog through the night, and the next day, when Bill came to check up on them, he found Andrea giving the pit bull a bath and singing, "Gonna wash those fleas right outta your hair."

Bill fell with a splash.

And animals have been a part of their happily-ever-after ever since.

When God means for two people to be together for life, nothing can stand in the way. Not even nose voltage, ice packs, drunk puppies, or PMS.

> *[Love] always protects, always trusts, always hopes, always perseveres. Love never fails.*
>
> 1 CORINTHIANS 13:7–8

2

Romantically Impaired

An examination of this (mostly) male disability.
For instance, women like lots of words,
while men prefer sticking to single syllables.

MOST GUYS AREN'T TOO GOOD with words—especially on a volume scale.

But hey, it's not their fault.

It's genetic.

A recent scientific study said that women use about a gazillion words a day, while men use only four.

And words, to many women, equal romance.

"My boyfriend is romantically impaired," sighed Elisabeth, a single woman from Colorado. "His most difficult area is with words. . . .

"In one of our discussions on how he could be more romantic, I reminded him once again that women love compliments," she said. "He responded that he complimented me all the time, and proceeded to list a few that had occurred within the past couple of days.

"Yes," she told him, "but you said the same thing every time! You said I looked good. I begin to think you don't mean it if you say the same thing every time. Why don't you ever say anything different? Like, comment on the specifics. Why don't you ever say I'm beautiful?"

With a straight face and in all sincerity, this man said, "Too many syllables."

Syllables. Words.

See what I mean?

Genetic.

Then there was the married woman who said her husband didn't talk a lot, but she does. (Sounds familiar.) Anyway, their fifteenth wedding anniversary was approaching, and she came up with the idea that fifteen days before the anniversary they would both start telling each other the things they were thankful for about the other.

The first day of this fifteen-day love fest, her husband gave her a big hug, looked deeply into her eyes and said, "I really admire you."

Four words.

Short, sweet, and to the point.

But leaning just a smidge toward romantically challenged.

His wife wanted specifics. (Hint: Guys, we love details. Ever wonder why we have such lengthy phone conversations with our girlfriends? It's all in the details.)

Then there are those actions that, as the saying goes, "speak louder than words."

One woman—I'll call her Maggie—said that all of her old flames were romantically impaired (which is why she's still single).

"One guy only held my hand when we were in a crushing crowd—so he wouldn't lose me," Maggie said. "Also, he would only take me places that were free—like fireworks—and we couldn't park the car until after six P.M. because that's when you no longer have to feed the meters.

"He brought a can of pop each and a bag of chips for the two of us to share.

"He also brought his sister and her girlfriend along— AAARRRRGGGHHH!

"When he finally took me to dinner—just the two of us—he called it a business expense and put it on his corporate card," Maggie concluded. "Did I feel special or what? And was this a date? I ditched him too soon to find out—and this was the guy I'd hoped was Mr. Right."

My reporter friend, Patty Reyes Humphrey, said that before she met her "incredibly romantic husband," Rob (whom she says God made just to her specifications), she had dated another guy for three years who started out as quite the romantic.

This guy always gave Patty presents on special occasions: birthdays, Valentine's Day, even month-to-month anniversaries.

However, as the relationship progressed, the gifts became less romantic and more practical—"homemaker-like"—a coffee maker, a hand vacuum. . . .

One Valentine's Day she bought him a nice watch.

Then it was her turn.

She began opening her gift, growing more and more excited with anticipation as she tore into the wrapping paper . . .

As the last of the shimmery wrapping hit the floor, so did her jaw.

A socket wrench set.

As she pulled out the wrenches one by one, no matter how hard she tried to imagine what he had in mind—even a tire gauge would have been more useful—it still remained a set of socket wrenches.

They broke up shortly after that.

But let's be fair about this. It's not only men who are romantically impaired.

There was the woman who invited all their wedding guests to the honeymoon hotel—on the wedding night—so the reception could continue on into the evening.

Her husband had a slightly more private reception in mind.

Another woman was cleaning off her husband's desk one day when she found a dirty old rock in the midst of his things, which she promptly threw in the trash.

When her husband returned home that night, he was dismayed to find the rock missing. The "dirty old rock" his wife had thrown out was one he'd picked up from the beach the day they walked along the shore and first declared their love for each other.

Although being romantically challenged is more of a

gender-neutral disability, I suggest that there is one handicap peculiar to men:

The birthday impairment.

Some men, deeply in love with their wife or girlfriend, are just a little birthday-impaired.

For instance, one woman said that early in their marriage, after they'd bought their first house, she and her husband agreed to not buy each other Christmas or birthday gifts that year.

Instead, they would put all their money toward the house.

However, on her birthday, her husband walked in with a gigantic wrapped box. She was secretly thrilled, thinking, *How sweet! He got me a birthday present anyway.*

As she excitedly ripped off the wrapping paper, she was imagining all the treasures such a huge box could hold.

But when the last of the paper fell away, she looked dumbfounded at a brand-new toilet.

Not the most romantic of gifts. (But definitely practical.)

Another woman I know is married to a really great guy who adores her and treats her like a queen. Periodically he surprises her—and makes all her female coworkers jealous—by having a dozen roses delivered to her at work.

However, as terrific as this sounds, he, too, suffers from the birthday impairment disability—he never has a clue what to get her for a birthday present.

So they've worked out a deal: She buys her own birthday present and tells him later what he gave her. (The only problem is, sometimes he forgets, so when they're on their way to some friends' house to celebrate her birthday, he'll say, "Now tell me again what I got you—just in case they ask.")

Then there are the forgetful types.

Ana says that on their second Valentine's Day together, her husband forgot the holiday—even though he insists he didn't.

"I later confirmed my suspicion," she says, "when I opened the beautiful card he'd given me and it said, 'To my dear grandmother on Valentine's Day.'"

Impaired? Maybe. But you still gotta love 'em.

I liken you, my darling, to a mare harnessed to one of the chariots of Pharaoh. Your cheeks are beautiful with earrings, your neck with strings of jewels. We will make you earrings of gold, studded with silver.

SONG OF SONGS 1:9–11

3

Flying Food and Other First Date Disasters

You're at a nice restaurant having a lovely dinner with the man of your dreams . . . when suddenly a cherry tomato you've just bitten into squirts seeds all over your date's cheek.

ON HER FIRST DATE with this good-looking guy in college, the nervous young co-ed really wanted to make a good impression.

They went out for hamburgers, but as she dipped her head down to sip her soda, the straw went up her nose instead. She lifted her head, thinking the straw would just fall out.

Instead, it dangled from her nostril for all to see.

She quickly yanked out the straw, but all was lost.

The good-looking guy never asked her out again.

First dates can be pretty nerve-wracking, especially when they're with someone you *really* like. You're nervous and you want everything to be just perfect, but all too often that nervousness translates into disaster.

Take my girlfriend Katie, who was so excited as she got ready for her first date with a guy named Mark that she sprayed perfume in her mouth instead of breath freshener.

On a subsequent date with Mark, they'd gone to a wedding together and she wanted to dance at the reception.

He didn't.

So, just for fun, she convinced her twin sister to dance with her instead.

They were having a grand old time, laughing and really getting into the music. But then, right in the midst of their sisterly shimmying, her slip fell off.

That didn't stop Mark from marrying her. (Although her sister has yet to dance with her again.)

Probably my worst-ever first date disaster happened when I was stationed in England.

A nice, sweet air force captain had invited me to his squadron party—a rather formal affair that was made up of mostly officers and their wives.

As a young enlisted woman, I knew I couldn't compete with the expensive gowns the officers' wives were sure to be wearing. So I scoured the local shops until I managed to find the perfect dress—an elegant, spaghetti-strapped royal blue evening gown with matching wrap—marked down 50 percent—that managed to just fit into my "enlisted" budget.

Unfortunately, the evening didn't begin very auspiciously—on *my* part.

When my date arrived to pick me up, I firmly informed him that I was a feminist and therefore didn't believe in all that "old-fashioned opening the door for me stuff," so he was *NOT* to open any doors for me or take my arm to guide me across the street or anything chauvinistic like that. (This was the late '70s, during my young, impressionable "I am woman, hear me roar" days, when I obnoxiously mistook courtesy and good manners for male oppression.)

However, my date had been raised to be a gentleman, so treating women as ladies was innately bred into him, and he didn't take my command seriously. Consequently, we spent the first part of the evening trying to outrace each other to the door to open it.

But that wasn't the worst part.

No, that came at the end of the evening.

We were standing near the door getting ready to leave and talking to a group of his buddies, when his squadron commander came over—a full bird colonel. We chatted for a couple of minutes, but I felt uncomfortable because the colonel's eyes kept straying to my chest.

I was rather surprised and offended by this inappropriate gaze, especially from a commanding officer, when suddenly I felt a draft.

Wondering where the chill was coming from, I glanced down and to my horror discovered why the colonel's attention kept wandering. One of the spaghetti straps on my brand-new bargain dress had slipped off my shoulder, taking with it that entire side of my bodice.

Talk about northern exposure.

Dying of mortification, but not wanting to call further attention to my predicament, I casually gathered my wrap around my shoulders, holding it together firmly in the front.

This time, as we made our way back to my date's car, I let him open the door—since both of my hands were otherwise occupied.

Then there's the woman who went to an expensive French restaurant on a first date.

She was nervously fiddling with her fork when she accidentally dropped it. The waiter quickly appeared with a clean one, which she directly dropped in the same manner. The waiter very patiently brought her another fork. But when her jittery fiddling caused her to drop a third fork, the waiter handed her another with the comment, "Perhaps Madam would like a rubber band?"

Fortunately, her date had a good sense of humor and they dated for about a year. (Until she dropped him, too.)

A woman I know—I'll call her Jennifer—told me of the time she was sitting at the table with her new boyfriend while he ate. All of a sudden, in the middle of chewing his food, he coughed. The next thing she knew, food was streaming out of his nose!

Jennifer kept talking as if nothing happened. At the time she was working with children and was pretty accustomed to kids' gross eating habits. (The incident, by the way, didn't gross her out badly enough to prevent her from marrying the guy.)

It could have been worse.

Like the time I bit into a cherry tomato and the seeds squirted all over my date's face.

He decided to skip the dancing cheek-to-cheek he'd planned for later.

My friend Annie Jornlin said that her first date ever was with a guy who had "excellent dimples."

"My best friend was supposed to double-date with us," Annie said, "but at the last minute her parents wouldn't let her go."

That's how Annie wound up at a drive-in with two guys.

One (Dimple Man) spilled popcorn all over them, and the other guy brought his trumpet and played it most of the evening in the car. (If I'd been the friend left behind, I think I'd have thanked my parents for not letting me go!)

Then there's a couple from our church, Quenten and Doris Goldstein, who met and began dating in high school.

Doris said she knew pretty quickly that Quenten was "the one" and that God meant for them to be together, but Quenten wasn't quite as sure. Whenever they got what he deemed "too serious," she said he would try to date other girls.

He tried three times. And each time got into an auto accident prior to the date (giving new meaning to "First Date Disaster").

"He finally got the message, and I didn't have to do a thing," said Doris.

They've been married twenty-six years—without any major fender-benders.

He who began a good work in you will carry it on to completion until the day of Christ Jesus.

PHILIPPIANS 1:6

4

Every Knight's Armor Has Rust

*Yes, Virginia, there can be a Mr. Right,
just not a Mr. Perfect,
so throw away that shopping list!*

Chicken	Chocolate
Rice	Kleenex
Broccoli	*Compassionate*
Tall	Midol
Bread	*College-Educated*
Milk	Steak
Sensitive	Mushrooms
Romantic	*Has a job!*

Looking-for-Mr.-Right lists begin in childhood.

As my little friends and I played with our dolls, they all imagined themselves as the beautiful, buxom Barbie, longing to grow up and marry someone just like Ken.

Not me.

He was a little too blond, bland, and beach-blown for my taste. (Although Mattel® must have seen the light, because Ken now has dark hair.) I preferred the more "intellectual" type. That's why my very first Mr. Perfect list read "tall, dark, and smart."

As the girls of my generation grew older, we all fell for TV heroes—kind of like the preteens today with their *Party of Five* crushes. But our tastes ran to the more mature and sophisticated ... like "Little Joe" Cartwright.

In the mid-'60s, weekly TV Westerns were the best place to find a plethora of handsome hunks.

Bonanza was my favorite.

And not just because of the curly-haired, mischievous and absolutely adorable "Little Joe" either. Some episodes I was also drawn to the dark-haired, handsome Adam who always dressed in black and was so wise and mature. (Although, what was the deal with their clothes?

As rich as the Ponderosa was, you'd think they could have afforded more than one outfit!)

There were even times that I fell for Hoss. (Hey, for such a big guy, he was dad-burned gentle and a girl would sure feel safe around him.)

Of course, my preferences changed weekly depending on which one of the boys was taking a girl for a buggy ride and a picnic. But did you ever notice that going on a picnic with one of the Cartwright boys usually ended in death for the unlucky woman of the week? That's why I scratched that romantic scenario and moved on to the Barkley brothers over at *The Big Valley*.

The only problem was, not one of them alone had all the characteristics on my wish list.

I yearned for the intelligence of Jarrod, the strength of Nick, and the sensitivity of Heath. (Of course, later Heath became "The Six-Million-Dollar Man," so I could have had two out of three in one package, if I'd only known.)

As we grew up, many of us carried this perfect Knight-in-Shining-Armor list into our twenties and thirties—making it a little difficult when we were confronted with reality and men who were just as imperfect as we were. When I became a Christian in my late twenties, I just amended my list a bit to include: "godly-man-who-loves-the-Lord-and-will-love-me-the-way-Christ-loved-the-church."

I still remember my first ever singles retreat at Lake Tahoe, a few days shy of my thirtieth birthday. I was surrounded by God's majesty in California's breathtaking Sierra Nevada mountains with that clear, crisp, high-elevation air that takes your breath away—especially after climbing the steep hill to the dining hall.

It was a perfect place to pray and reflect and focus on the Lord and seek His will.

The first night during the get-to-know-one-another session, I found myself one of a quartet of single women between the ages of twenty-nine and thirty-one. We'd all been Christians less than three years, and as we reveled in the Lord's creation in that glorious, spiritual environment, we were all excited to share what God had been doing in our lives.

"So what are you looking for in a man?" one of the women asked.

"I want someone who's attractive, intelligent, fun, and likes kids," said the redheaded, slim-hipped single mom who worked as a disc jockey.

"I'm interested in the double-breasted, leather-sole kind of a guy with a sense of humor and who loves to dance," said the woman who worked in the shoe department at Macy's. "But only during the week. On the weekends, he'd be the Marlboro man."

"I'd like to meet someone who's strong yet sensitive, and who loves the Lord and would be a good spiritual leader," said the woman who'd been a Christian the longest.

"I just want a man who reads," I said.

A few minutes later, the blond, good-looking guitar player, who'd led the evening's worship, sauntered over to say hello. That's when my newfound friends pounced on him with the question, "Do you read?" (He did, but he only had eyes for the redheaded deejay, whom he later married.)

There was a period in my life, however, when I didn't have a list. When I had been hurt so deeply that I didn't even believe in such a thing as a Mr. Right. As far as I was concerned, men were all Mr. Wrongs. They were just predators who devastated and destroyed.

My destruction began when I was raped at the age of eighteen.

From that moment on, I had a difficult time trusting men. I saw them only through cynical, dark-colored glasses.

For instance, there was Harry-the-Hit-Man, who hit on every woman in sight—single and married; and Freddie-the-Flatterer, who told you that you were the most beautiful woman he'd ever seen — until a new flavor-of-the-week turned up.

Then there was Lying Larry, who promised to call but never did; and Bachelor Bill — what GIs stationed overseas called a Class B bachelor — whose wife was home in the States.

But thankfully, that angry male-bashing season of my life has passed. After years of hoping that someday my prince would come (and winding up with a bunch of frogs instead), the Lord brought me the Mr. Right He intended for me all along.

He knows so clearly what we need.

Many are the plans in a [wo]man's heart, but it is the Lord's purpose that prevails.

PROVERBS 19:21

5

Prayer in the Parking Lot

Or how an innocent three-hour conversation and prayer in a parking lot late at night can turn a not-so-young woman's thoughts to love and marriage.

OF ALL THE SINGLES GROUPS in all the churches in all the towns in all the world, he walks into mine.

It was early on a Friday night when he ambled into the Sunday School room to join the singles session already in progress. I watched him surreptitiously from beneath my lowered Lauren Bacall lids as he made his way down the rows of nondescript metal folding chairs to a seat on the far side of the room.

Once there, he stashed his *NIV Study Bible* beneath his chair and promptly joined in the chorus of "I Love You, Lord."

As I discreetly gazed at his radiant, upturned face, closed eyes, and hands raised in adoration, I was filled with one consuming thought: how much I wanted to kiss his eyelids.

And I know I wasn't alone in this desire. The room was filled with dozens of single, spiritual women, and as I looked around me, it seemed as if every pair of feminine eyes was focused on him.

"Back off," I warned them silently. "I saw him first."

As I halfheartedly listened to the evening's sermon, I began imagining a romantic relationship of uncommon depth with this good-looking, godly man.

I could envision our taking walks in the park as we shared deep, spiritual insights. For instance, in the Mary and Martha story, was Mary really intent on listening to Jesus or did she just not like to do housework? And was that burning bush deciduous or evergreen? These were questions that had plagued humankind for centuries, and together, perhaps, we could find the answers.

In addition to solving these biblical mysteries, we could also flex our intellectual muscles by sparring over the profundities of Francis Schaeffer and C. S. Lewis. Or maybe we'd go downtown and pass out evangelistic tracts together and he'd see what a heart I had for the lost.

I had our whole relationship mapped out but I wasn't quick enough.

Before the "men" in Amen was barely out of my mouth, a small cluster of women had already circled this tall, dark, and handsome bachelor with the great eyelids. However, I had an "in" that they didn't. We'd already had a conversation the week before, so that meant I had a prior claim. And if that didn't work, as one of the members of the Singles Leadership Hospitality team, it was important that I fulfill my duties as Holly Hospitality.

As the evening drew to a close, a few of us stayed behind to put away chairs and clean up the cookie crumbs and lipstick-rimmed Styrofoam coffee cups that littered the room. From out of the corner of my eye, I made sure I kept pace with "Eyelid Man" so that when he was finished and getting ready to leave, so was I.

Big surprise.

As he walked me to my car on that cold November evening, we got into a deep philosophical discussion about life, God, doctrine, and dating.

Half an hour later we agreed to continue the conversation in my car since the wind was slicing through us. Before long, the windows were all fogged up—not from necking! (We were Christians after all, and we were sitting in the church parking lot.) But more to the point, he had told me he wasn't interested in me in "that way."

But as the night turned into morning and still we kept on talking, I began to sense that the tide was turning and perhaps he was interested in me after all. We'd already covered predestination, spiritual gifts, feeding the hungry, and celibacy. How could he not be interested?

After all, I was a witty, well-read, godly woman complete with a colorful testimony. (Besides, we'd been sitting in my cold, cramped car for more than two hours already. And I didn't let my fingers go numb with cold for just anyone!)

However, the real clincher came an hour later when we prayed together.

Nothing could have been more romantic. Especially to a reformed sinner whose prior experience with prayer had been pretty well limited to "Now-I-Lay-Me-Down-to-Sleep" or "Our-Father-Who-Art-in-Heaven." There I was, sitting in my old white Toyota with a broken heater at three A.M. in near-freezing weather—with a former missionary-from-Africa, no less—having an in-depth and heartfelt conversation with God.

I wondered if missionary-man-with-the-great-eyelids would want to have our wedding in Africa?

He didn't . . . sigh.

I wasn't the only one perplexed by the parking-lot-prayer conundrum. I remember one good friend of mine, a real "WOG" (woman of God, as some of the guys referred to her admiringly), in her mid-thirties, who'd been a Christian since her teens. She was well-loved and respected by all who knew her. She'd even spent time on the mission field.

But she suffered from the same single spiritual syndrome as I did.

"Every Friday night," she said, "there'd be the last few of us cleaning up and we'd walk outside together and talk. First there would be four people talking, then three, and then just the two of us. We'd talk about everything . . . politics, God, gardening . . . and I'd think, *Oh, he likes flowers and gardens. What a poetic, sensitive guy.*

"He could spend hours talking and it was just so comfortable. We'd sit in the car and just relax. Then we'd pray.

"Wow! Holding hands while you pray—that's the big one. All those feelings of warmth; mental, emotional, and spiritual.

"But then we'd leave and go our separate ways."

Parking-lot prayer has its genesis inside the church.

Before I became a Christian, I was always "Lookin' for Love in All the Wrong Places," but once I became one, I started looking for love in all the RIGHT places.

One such right place was in the small prayer groups at Singles. Men were much more apt to open up and share their feelings there and allow us to see their vulnerable side. (Something that just reduces all of us womenfolk to a pile of mush.) Also, prayer groups gave the men a chance to see you at your most spiritual—especially if you were an eloquent pray-er.

There was one night when I'd been fervently praying for someone in the group when the guy next to me—whom I naturally had a crush on—grabbed my hands and asked me to pray for something "really important." For a few brief seconds, I fantasized that we might reenact the scene in *The Quiet Man* when John Wayne grabs Maureen O'Hara, pulls her to him, and kisses her passionately. . . .

But my romantic reverie was rudely cut short when the guy asked for prayer for his brand-new fiancée.

I just hate it when reality intrudes on romance.

The next Friday night, when a dashing Rhett Butler-kind-of-a-guy acted like he frankly didn't give a hoot about my Scarlett O'Hara-style of Christian coquetry, I decided that I wouldn't think about it that night. I'd think about it tomorrow.

After all, as that great *Gone with the Wind* theologian once said, "Tomorrow is another day."

He who pursues righteousness and love finds life,
prosperity and honor.

PROVERBS 21:21

6

"Touch My Ankle, You'd Better Marry Me!

Why some maidens pucker up to the "no-kissing" rule, while others draw the line at the top of their high-buttoned boots.

THE FIRST TIME I VISITED a large Christian singles group, I was shocked by what I witnessed: men and women touching each other right there in front of God and everybody! My face flushed scarlet and I had to quickly turn my eyes away. I wanted to leave immediately, but just at that moment, the pastor began to pray.

I prayed too.

Lord, I said silently, *Help that couple to keep their hands to themselves and to focus on you. Amen.* But when I opened my eyes, they hadn't stopped and they were directly in my line of vision! And nobody else seemed to notice. . . . HOW could that be? Was I the only Pollyanna Pure in the bunch?

The singles pastor kept right on preaching, while all the time the guy five rows in front of me continued to give the girl next to him . . .

A BACK RUB!

I know, I know. To many it's just an innocent tension reliever, but those are usually the ones who became Christians while still in the womb. For those of us who weren't born again until much later in life and had had more than our share of not-so-innocent back rubs, it could be a huge stumbling block.

Which for me, the former Polly-Promiscuous-before-God-restored-my-virginity-as-a-new-creation-in-Christ, it was.

However, I soon realized that my reaction was just a little to the right of radical and that most people did not share my view.

In fact, many did not even understand it (including the touchy-feely kind of creepy guy who would come up behind a woman and start rubbing her neck without an invitation).

He only did it to me once.

In a very loving and Christlike manner, I explained to him that I didn't like that kind of contact; I considered it inappropriate and I would prefer that he not do it again. "So get your slimy hands off me, dirtbag!" (Actually, I only said that in my mind . . . it was the karate chop and headlock that really clued him in.)

But I have plenty of very virginal and pure Christian friends who believe that back rubs are fine. In fact, one group of women friends has even developed their own set of rules for physical contact between men and women before marriage:

- Hand holding and back rubs are okay.
- Kissing doesn't come until you're engaged, or at least in an exclusive relationship that almost certainly will wind up at the altar.

I made up my own set of rules:

- No back rubs.
- No hand holding (unless one of the hands is sprouting a glittery growth on the left ring finger)!
- No kissing unless you're ready to back it up with a proposal.
- Touch my ankle, you'd better marry me!

Many people don't realize it, but ankles were once considered quite the turn-on for men. In fact, men have been known to fight duels over a glimpse of a well-turned ankle. (That's why women used to wear long dresses and high-buttoned shoes, so as not to incite a riot.) I wanted to post a very clear Hands Off sign to the men at Singles. Well, it worked . . . only too well.

I didn't have a date for nearly five years.

But at least I was in good company.

By then I'd discovered Elisabeth Elliot's *Passion and Purity*,* which tells of the love story between her and Jim

---

*Elisabeth Elliot, *Passion and Purity* (Grand Rapids, Mich.: Fleming H. Revell, a division of Baker Book House Company, 1984), 11, 39.

Elliot in the late '40s through the mid-'50s—a love that had been brought "under the authority of Christ" and that "stayed out of bed" until the wedding night.

It became my bulwark, my guide, and my measuring stick for any possible future relationship. It also effectively became the death knell for any relationship in my singles group because all the guys thought I was some kind of weirdo.

"What do you mean—no kissing until you're engaged? That's (fill-in-the-blank) archaic, extreme, ridiculous, old-fashioned. . . ." (This was usually said to me by men who expected or demanded a good-night kiss at the end of a first date.)

But that wasn't for me. I wanted to hold out.

Besides, it seemed to me that casual kissing just to be kissing makes it as common as the everyday handshake.

Of course, I watched countless grooms kiss countless brides and longed for the day when my lips would be joined with another's in a matrimonial mouth lock. (A kiss may be "just a kiss," but when you haven't had one in years, the desire to pucker can become pretty potent.) I lived vicariously through those nuptial kisses, then went home and prayed for endurance.

Then I attended the Urbana Missions Conference in Illinois. There I met a couple of intelligent, attractive women nearly ten years younger than I who'd grown up in the church. I eagerly shared my kissless dating philosophy with them, but they both dismissed it as completely unrealistic for this day and age. To them, and many others, I was simply filled with all the zeal and passion of a new convert—something that I wouldn't be able to sustain over the long haul.

And they were right.

I wish I could say I fought the good fight to the end, but I have to confess that after almost five years of maintaining this strong, righteous stance, I faltered.

I backslid briefly when I returned to college in my early thirties.

I was mad at God for not bringing me a mate after

all my years of faithfulness, so when I ran into a sweet guy from my old singles group whom I'd had a major crush on, I happily accepted his invitation to dinner.

A wonderful meal and a couple of hours later, we were standing out in his backyard looking up at the stars, when all of a sudden, WHAM—we kissed.

And you know what? I thoroughly enjoyed it. Plus, I knew it meant something. I mean, after all, it HAD to— after that long a wait.

Time to break out *Bride* magazine and the birdseed. Right.

A few days later we went to see a movie, and he even held my hand! I just KNEW we were in sync down the same romantic path.

Not exactly.

I was disappointed and hurt to discover that our expectations and the meanings we attached to physical contact were quite different.

But we later talked through the hurt and he apologized and asked for my forgiveness.

I knew that I wanted a "relationship" to go along with the kisses and the hand holding. So when we parted that day, I left my brother in Christ with the gentle caution to be careful with his hands and lips because I knew I wasn't the only Christian woman longing for a mate who would read something more into it. ("Do not arouse or awaken love until it so desires" [Song of Songs 2:7].)

For me, a few kisses and some hand holding awakened love.

There is no set rule or clearly drawn line anymore.

Actually, there wasn't when Jim and Elisabeth Elliot were courting more than forty-five years ago either. As she says in *Passion and Purity*,* "Our Christian contemporaries were necking in cars ('scrunching' was the current word in our college), holding hands on campus, kissing in the dormitory lounges. When speakers came to campus, the question students always asked was

---

*Elisabeth Elliot, *Passion and Purity*, 125.

where to draw the line, how far could they go?"

That same question is being asked today, and everyone is answering it differently.

Even though I faltered briefly, I knew that I couldn't kiss, hold hands, or have my ankles touched until God's choice for me was ready to back it up with a marriage proposal.

Less than a year later, it was love's time—God's time—for me.

He brought me a self-controlled, godly man who did not want the physical side of a relationship to cloud his thinking or the Lord's leading, so we had a very chaste courtship. The day he finally held my hand, I went home and thanked the Lord!

This man did not even kiss me until the night he proposed. (Although that was a mere six weeks after we started dating.)

Of course, when he asked me to marry him, what were the first words out of my mouth? "Now you HAVE to kiss me!"

So we kissed, and he held me in his arms for the first time. I was completely content.

"Well?" he asked.

"Well, what?" I replied, nestling my head deeper into the crook in his shoulder.

"You haven't answered my question."

"Oh—yes, of course I'll marry you."

Do not arouse or awaken love until it so desires.

SONG OF SOLOMON 2:7

7

"Can I Flirt, or Will I Lose My Salvation?"

*Can Christians flirt? I thought
the eleventh commandment was
"Thou shalt not flirt."*

AMY CARMICHAEL, BELOVED missionary to India, was not known for her flirting prowess.

Neither was prolific hymn composer Fanny Crosby.

Scarlett O'Hara, on the other hand, was the ultimate flirt.

With one flutter of her eyelashes, she'd have men from three counties eating out of her hand. However, she's not exactly a Proverbs 31 role model.

Christianity and flirting just don't go hand in hand.

That's because real Christians don't flirt. (It's the eleventh commandment, I've heard.)

But for those of us who learned to bat our eyelashes with the best of them when we were "in the world," it's a tough commandment to keep.

As a "baby" Christian, I tried hard to live up to the image of what a godly woman should be.

One thing she most definitely was not, was a flirt.

At least that's what I thought until I met little "Sharlene" from Texas.

Sharlene was sweet, young, and pretty, had just graduated from a prestigious Christian college, and had a bewitching Texas drawl that lassoed every man in sight from sixteen to sixty.

She was also smart, funny, and my friend.

Out of the blue, men were suddenly inviting me to a whole slew of events and activities that I'd never been privy to before—along with Sharlene, of course.

But the event that has to go down in flirting history was a fishing trip we took with a couple of die-hard single outdoorsmen in their mid-thirties.

Now, I have never been—and never will be—the outdoorsy type.

Sure, I enjoy a walk through the woods with "Walden," backyard barbecues, or a picnic beside a cool mountain stream, but that's about the extent of my outside activity.

However, the idea of getting away to a quiet cabin at beautiful Lake Tahoe was just too tempting to pass up, so I gamely agreed to go along. Besides, the guys were both friends from Singles leadership (and cute to boot).

The cabin was everything I'd dreamed of and more.

The fishing trip, on the other hand, wasn't.

My first clue that it wasn't going to be quite the idyllic weekend I'd envisioned came on the drive up Highway 50 when Sharlene kept up a steady patter of wide-eyed questions about fishing that had each John Wayne-wannabe trying to outdo the other impressing her with his Marlin Perkins knowledge.

The next hint arrived the following morning when we had to wake up at the crack of dawn—something I hadn't experienced since my basic training days.

Thankfully, the guys weren't as abrupt as the military dorm guard who would snap on the light and loudly bark, "It is now 0500 hours. All airmen will be up, all airmen will be awake."

Instead, they gently rapped on our door and softly said, "Time to get up, girls."

Sharlene and I pulled on some warm clothes, applied a dash of lipstick (that woman never went anywhere without her lipstick), ate a quick breakfast, then drove to the local bait shop where the men bought a bunch of greasy, grimy worms.

After arriving at the guys' favorite fishing spot, we all hunkered down with our gear, preparing to cast off and reel in some big ones.

I was busily untangling my fishing line when I heard Sharlene say, "Could one of y'all help me with this li'l ol' worm?" They nearly capsized the boat in their eagerness to be of assistance to the lovely Sharlene.

And I was left squeamishly holding a Styrofoam cup of squiggly, wiggly worms poking their heads up through the dirt. (Do worms even have heads? One end looks pretty much like another to me.)

"Hel-lo-o-o-w," I said in my best Billy Crystal impression. "Could I have some help, too?"

"Be with you in just a minute," one of my plaid-shirted pals said.

At that moment I finally realized that my function on the weekend getaway was to serve as chaperone (or referee) between the guys for Sharlene's affections.

But since I'd left my whistle and black-and-white striped shirt at home, I decided the next day I'd hang out at the cabin and go fishin' with Andy and Opie instead.

I didn't blame Sharlene, though.

It wasn't her fault that she turned grown men into a pile of mush. Scarlett had the same effect.

I imitated Sharlene's technique once or twice, but when you're tall enough to stand shoulder to shoulder with a man, it just doesn't engender the same protective attitude as when you're five-foot-two-with-eyes-of-blue. (Could also have something to do with my nasal Wisconsin accent. I think flirting loses something in that Midwest translation.)

Besides, I tried a southern drawl once, but it came out sounding more like Ma Kettle than Scarlett O'Hara.

Not quite the honeyed cadence I was striving for.

That's when I hung up my false eyelashes and decided flirting must not be a godly pursuit.

But old habits die hard.

Occasionally, when I'd find myself talking to some great guy, I'd slip into automatic coquette mode where my eyelashes took on a mind of their own—a fluttery one—no matter how hard I tried to harness them.

At this rate, I was sure to lose my salvation.

But women are not the only ones well-versed in the art of flirting.

In fact, some men could even give lessons.

There was one drop-dead gorgeous guy who had the ability to make every woman he met feel as if she was the most beautiful, interesting, intelligent woman on the face of the earth and that no other woman existed.

So it was quite a heady feeling when that hunka burnin' love came over and focused his undivided attention—and his beautiful baby blues—on me.

That man really knew how to flirt.

The only problem was, he was so good at it that some women (including yours truly) mistook it for more than it really was and wound up with hurt feelings.

If he'd just batted his baby blues at me, and maybe even giggled once or twice, I'd have realized it was just friendly, fun-loving flirting—that didn't mean a thing. But under his steady, unblinking gaze, I fell headfirst.

Katie could have taught him a thing or two.

But I didn't realize that when I first met her. All I knew was that she was petite, had curly blond hair, giggled a lot, and was the biggest flirt around.

Bar none.

What I didn't know was that she was also smart, funny, kind, and one of the most godly women I'd ever met.

She led small-group Bible studies, discipled and counseled countless women, and was always willing to help anyone in need.

But she also flirted. A lot. And didn't see the harm in it.

"It's fun to flirt," she'd say, giggling.

That's when I learned that flirting and godliness are not mutually exclusive.

Besides, I've looked and looked, and nowhere in the Bible can I find that eleventh commandment: Thou shalt not flirt. (Maybe I just don't have the right translation.)

A cheerful look brings joy to the heart.

PROVERBS 15:30

8

"A Norwegian From Wisconsin? He Must Be God's Choice for Me.

I'm a Norwegian from Wisconsin, too!"

AS A YOUNG GIRL of strong Norwegian stock growing up in Racine, Wisconsin, I never even considered falling in love with someone from the "Dairy state."

Not me.

Instead, I yearned to be swept off my feet by an exciting, cosmopolitan, well-traveled "man of the world."

I dreamed of living in a world-class city like London or Paris where I would meet tall, dark, intellectual men at sophisticated dinner parties as a result of my glamorous, globe-trotting profession as a foreign correspondent.

We'd indulge in stimulating rounds of witty repartee a la Rosalind Russell and Cary Grant in *His Girl Friday*, or Grace Kelly and Cary in *To Catch a Thief*.

Well, I did globe-trot—to London, Paris, Amsterdam, and Athens—but not as a foreign correspondent. Instead, I flew a typewriter in the U.S. Air Force.

And I did meet some men. Some of whom were even tall and dark. Or short and intelligent. But none of whom was quite Mr. Right—although I thought so at least once.

A few years later when I became a Christian, I thought I'd found that perfect guy—the first single man I met at the first Christian singles group I ever attended. Not only was he single and a Christian, he also had a beard (a prominent item on my "Mr. Right" checklist)!

As a brand-new, "baby" Christian, I thought I'd hit the jackpot.

Instead, I wound up broke (Emotionally, that is).

After this breakup (a week before we were to marry) I took my bruised and battered heart to a Bible study at a different church—where I wouldn't run into my ex-fiancé—so that I could heal and become better acquainted with God's Word.

What a fabulous Bible study! I learned so much. And the preacher was so on fire for the Lord too. You could tell he had a very close walk with God because he absolutely emanated the love of Christ.

He also had a beard and was single.

But God was to show me that there was more to a relationship than that.

Through that study, I matured and grew in the Lord and made friends with other women who'd been single Christians much longer than I. That's when I learned that my love life was no longer a gamble. God was now in control of it and I needed to let Him choose my mate.

I watched my godly girlfriends and learned all about seeking God's will in His choice for me.

One woman I knew was head over heels for another pastor-in-training.

She was completely convinced that he was God's choice for her. In fact, she said the Lord had "told" her that this man was going to be her husband. And she had a whole series of circumstances, incidents, and even Scriptures to back up this "promise."

I was impressed.

The only problem was, God forgot to tell the man, so he wound up marrying someone else. (Funny how it works that "both" people need to hear the call.)

This happened to a couple of other women I knew too.

But I knew it would never happen to me because *I* planned to let the Lord be in control. Far be it from me to manipulate or try to maneuver a potential romantic situation to my advantage.

Besides, I didn't even KNOW the bearded, single pastor.

I was just one of the multitude in his study. But I did know that he loved the Lord, and I heard that he was gentle and sweet and a wonderful counselor.

But most important of all, he read.

I peeked into his office once and it was wall-to-wall books. As a writer and voracious reader myself, this was critical.

Hey, God, are you trying to tell me something here?

After every Tuesday night Bible study, I'd go home and pray. *Lord, are you throwing Pastor Steve and I together like this because it's your will for us to be married? Lord, I give you this relationship. Please help me to listen to you and let you be in control.*

Occasionally, the very eligible Pastor Steve would make a casual comment about his desire to get married. This was further confirmation that he was God's choice for me.

After all, I wanted to get married too. Now I could really feel those holy hormones starting to rev up.

A few weeks later found me still praying. *Lord, if it's your will for Pastor Steve and I to marry, then I trust YOU to open the doors.*

One night after the study, I thought things were finally starting to happen when Pastor Steve walked over my way.

Yes, Lord! He's noticed my constant attendance and diligent note-taking week after week. And now he wants to talk to me over some of the more complex parts of tonight's text. Please help me not to sound too stupid. (And Lord, I wouldn't mind if he asked me out, either.)

With a friendly smile and warm brown eyes gazing into mine, the object of my affection extended his hand and said to me, "Hi, I'm Steve. Welcome. Are you new? I don't think I've seen you here before."

We chatted a couple of minutes, then he walked away to greet someone else—leaving my fingers still tingling from his touch.

"Hi, I'm Steve. Welcome . . ." he said to someone else (also a woman, but I couldn't tell if she was married or not, she was too far away for me to spot a ring).

But I still harbored secret hopes for our future together.

Eight months and many crushes later, my journal entry read, *Lord, what is this I feel for Pastor Steve? I don't even KNOW him. I just see his gentleness and kindness, and above all, his love for you and all these feelings start acting up in me.*

But eventually—a little more than a year after my fascination with Pastor Steve began (with no moves on his part toward a happily-ever-after with me)—another bearded man walked into my life.

Only this one was taller.

And Norwegian.

And from Wisconsin.

Gee, Lord, I guess I totally misread you on Pastor Steve, but now I know for sure that this is your choice for me. After all, we're from the same state and everything!

Finally, I realized that Pastor Steve was just a prelude to prepare me for my Wisconsin soulmate who'd also been to a few exotic places himself, like Africa—as a missionary, no less.

Talk about jackpot.

Over the next three years, this Norwegian bachelor from Wisconsin and I became close friends—further cementing the certainty I had that we were "made for each other."

He wasn't exactly on the same wavelength as I was on that one, however, but I was confident that given enough time he'd finally realize that God had made us for each other.

He never did.

Instead, he moved to the Lone Star state, where he later fell in love with and married a sweet Texas gal.

But by that point I didn't mind, because God had finally brought me the man he'd been holding for me all along: a native Californian who'd traveled to even more exotic places than I had with his job on a cruise ship.

Oh, and by the way, he had a beard, too.

I waited [im]patiently for the Lord; he turned to me and heard my cry.

PSALM 40:1

70

9

Honeymoon Horror Stories

*Or how to feel desirable when your toothbrush
and pretty peignoir are back in your
romantic honeymoon cabin
(while you're snowed in at the ski lodge).*

AFTER THE "I DO'S," most married couples are eager to get on their way and start the happily-ever-after part: the honeymoon.

Unfortunately, sometimes circumstances beyond their control—including Mother Nature and relatives—conspire to delay the happily-ever-after until *after* the honeymoon.

Take our friends Dana and Allan Loucks.

Much of their wedding night was spent entertaining a parade of hotel service personnel who traipsed in and out to fix their booby-trapped bridal suite. (Allan's brother Chris had borrowed the room key on the pretext of needing to get something.)

Finally, after the maintenance man screwed the light bulbs back in over the bathroom vanity, and the maids brought new sheets to replace the whipped-cream-covered ones on the bed, the bride and groom settled down for a very paranoid night's sleep.

But this was just the beginning of their honeymoon horror story.

They'd decided on a family vacation home at Lake Tahoe for their December honeymoon, but not wanting to get trapped in a snowdrift, chose to rent a four-by-four. Unfortunately for the style-conscious Allan, the only four-by-four available was a functional, albeit not very attractive, British Land Rover.

When they first arrived at their honeymoon haven, Allan shoveled lots and lots of snow so he and his bride could get in and out easily. Then they unpacked, put away groceries, and settled in for a week of bliss and relaxation.

Little did they know that the "Pineapple Express" was on its way.

This weather phenomenon from Hawaii (the worst weather in forty years) was a train of warm, tropic water that would melt the snow on the mountains at an exceptionally fast rate, causing the runoff to cross streets and go through garages and yards as it headed toward the lake.

One morning, the blissfully unaware newlyweds decided to venture into town for lunch.

As they approached a small village on their way to a restaurant renowned for its great burgers, they spotted a six-inch stream of water flowing across the road and into shops on the other side of the street.

Dana, the cautious, suggested that perhaps they should turn around and head back "home" to their honeymoon cabin instead of attempting to ford the stream.

But the single-task-oriented Allan, behind the wheel of his mighty, macho Land Rover—and really hungry for those burgers—decided to take the plunge.

Thankfully, they made it across and had a great lunch.

Which was a good thing, because it was one of the last enjoyable events of their honeymoon.

As they headed back toward what had earlier been a six-inch stream, they were stopped by a California Highway Patrolwoman who said they couldn't cross now because there was a four-foot-high wall of water coming down the mountain.

Allan argued that they might be able to make it across since, after all, they were in an all-terrain vehicle. However, the officer politely informed him that the other four-wheel drive vehicles who'd tried to cross had been swept off the road and were now floating in Lake Tahoe.

Two hours later found the not-so-happy couple— sans toothbrush, toothpaste, and a change of clothes— checking into the only available room at one of the hotel casinos in South Lake Tahoe (a smoking room).

Since Dana's allergic to smoke, she spent most of the

night sneezing and wheezing. (Not quite the romantic nirvana they'd envisioned.)

A day—and many more difficulties—later, when the unlucky couple heard that the "Pineapple Express" had passed, they decided to cut their honeymoon short and head for home.

But what they didn't know was that everyone else who'd been stranded up at Tahoe had the same idea. So they got stuck in a seven-and-a-half-hour traffic jam with thousands of other tourists.

Allan said he learned two valuable lessons from this experience:

"Never argue with a California Highway Patrol officer standing out in the rain, and trust your wife when she says, 'I don't think we should . . .'"

Chuck and Lynn had it easy compared to Dana and Allan.

They honeymooned in Costa Rica the week a major earthquake hit.

Friends and family back home were frantically trying to reach them after seeing frightening news reports on TV, but Chuck and Lynn were happily unaware of their concern. (Chuck still claims he was the one who made the earth move.)

Then there are the man-made honeymoon disasters.

Our neighbors Randy and Carol Allen honeymooned in Santa Cruz, California—renowned for its fabulous boardwalk and amusement-park atmosphere.

Naturally, Randy and Carol pigged out on some carnival junk food before heading for some tummy-tumbling amusement park rides—the last being the dreaded Octopus (the ride that goes round and round and up and down.)

Randy threw up first.

This grossed Carol out so much that she threw up too—all over her white pants.

At the end of the ride, the "carny" had to hose both of them off.

Then there were our other friends who spent part of their honeymoon in Reno. The husband got food poisoning and threw up all night long their first evening in the "biggest little city in the world."

A similar thing happened to me the second night of our honeymoon.

We were staying at a beautiful bed-and-breakfast in the southern Mendocino county town of Gualala. For a wedding gift, a friend had given us money specifically earmarked for an elegant dinner—which was a special treat for me because I love fine dining.

Michael wasn't really into the whole atmosphere and experience of fancy restaurants as much as I was—especially when he saw the cost: "This could buy us a whole day at Disneyland—including food and souvenirs!"

"Besides," he'd say oh-so-logically, "once you eat the food, it's gone. Then what do you have to show for all that money you've spent?"

But in this instance, since the dinner was a gift, he couldn't object.

Knowing this was a rare occasion, I went for the works: baked garlic and Brie, small Caesar salad, melt-in-my-mouth salmon, finished off by to-die-for chocolate mousse.

My taste buds thought they'd died and gone to heaven.

Unfortunately, my stomach wasn't in quite the same heavenly state.

Unaccustomed to so much rich food, it was now rebelling. I had to excuse myself from the table before even finishing my last spoonful of chocolate mousse.

Quickly—yet elegantly and unobtrusively—I made my way through the maze of tables filled with well-dressed men and perfectly coiffed women. Once I rounded the corner of the dining room into the hallway however, all elegance deserted me as I hiked up my skirt and sprinted up the stairs to the bathroom across from our room with a view.

When Michael came up a few minutes later, he found me curled up and groaning beneath the bedcovers.

Trying to be a tender and sympathetic husband, he laid down beside me and tried to hold me in his arms.

"Don't touch me!" I whimpered.

So much for romance.

But at least he didn't tell me that the meal was literally down the drain. (Not until we got home, that is.)

Curt and Peggy Clark had some pretty interesting dining experiences on their honeymoon too.

They were fairly naïve nineteen-year-olds when they got married—about a quarter of a century ago—and didn't understand the protocol or procedures of ordering room service at the very nice hotel where they stayed.

"Our first night there we decided to order a nice prime rib dinner brought to our little cottage on the hillside overlooking the ocean in Carmel," Peggy said. "The dinner itself cost approximately sixty dollars (including tip), so we left sixty dollars in cash on the tray when we were finished and set it outside our door.

"Not wanting to leave the comfort of our little cottage the next morning, we again ordered food in—the total this time coming to approximately twenty-five dollars. Again, we laid the cash out on the tray to be picked up."

It wasn't until they checked out and saw the cost of those meals tacked onto their bill that the newlyweds realized what big tippers they'd been.

"Fortunately, we had enough to pay the entire bill, but were too embarrassed to 'fess up to the hotel what went wrong," Peggy said.

Another one of my girlfriends is still too embarrassed to share the details of their honeymoon fiasco.

All she would say is, "It involves a Monterey bed-and-breakfast, a fire escape from the third floor, and us naked in the window."

Some say that a honeymoon horror story is a harbinger of a rocky marriage. I disagree. Instead, I think they are simply an example of how we are never truly in control of our circumstances.

Where you go I will go, and where you stay
I will stay. Your people will be my people
and your God my God.

RUTH 1:16

10

What We Have Here Is a Failure to Communicate

*I'll say something, knowing exactly what I mean,
but by the time it gets to his ears and through
his brain, somehow it means something
completely different.*

MICHAEL AND I OCCASIONALLY have communication problems.

I'm not sure why.

I'll say something, knowing exactly what I mean, but by the time it gets to his ears and through his brain, somehow it means something completely different.

Part of the problem is details.

I offer a lot, whereas Michael is from the "less is more" school.

He'll be telling me a story and out of the blue . . . "So, Joe said . . ."

I'll interrupt him and ask, "Who's Joe?" (since this is the first I've ever heard of him).

But he says I go to the other extreme.

When I'm telling a story and use someone's name, I always try to identify the person for the listener, so he or she can put it all in context. So I start something like, "Lana-my-best-friend-who-used-to-be-my-roommate-and-was-my-maid-of-honor . . ."

Another problem is assumptions.

For instance, Michael loves a good action/adventure movie, so recently, when the latest comic book hero adventure saga came out, being the thoughtful, considerate wife I am, I suggested that we go see it at our local movie house one evening.

Since movies are so expensive, we usually go to matinees, but I *knew* Michael really wanted to see this movie, so figured it would be a nice treat for him to go at night.

Afterward, however, we both agreed that the movie was pretty dreadful and we'd just wasted fifteen dollars.

"Oh well, honey, I knew you really wanted to see it,

so even though it was a bomb, you got to do something you wanted," I said.

Michael looked at me in surprise and said, "I only went because I thought *you* really wanted to see the movie!"

Talk about a failure to communicate.

It happens all the time in relationships.

For instance, when Katie and Mark were dating, she thought he might be giving her an engagement ring for her birthday.

Imagine her surprise when she opened her gift to find chocolate-covered pretzels and an apron that said, "You can never be too rich, too thin, or have too much chocolate," instead.

Less than a week later, she went to Mark's house for dinner.

He'd decided to cook a special meal for her, only he messed up on the measurements, mistakenly using tablespoons instead of teaspoons in the minestrone, so the soup was a little strong.

Then while he was cleaning up, the garbage disposal backed up, leaving potato peels, carrot peels, and onion skins floating in the sink.

Katie, having a sensitive stomach, sought shelter in the living room.

After Mark cleaned up the mess, he cleared his throat and said, "Katie, I have something serious I need to talk to you about."

She was convinced he was going to break up with her.

Instead, he proposed.

Then there was our first Valentine's Day in our new home.

We'd only been homeowners for a few months and had spent a lot of time and money—not to mention hour after hour of back-breaking labor—trying to make our fixer-upper habitable.

Since Michael and I both adore old movies, I thought it would be fitting and romantic to get him a copy of *Mr. Blandings Builds His Dream House* with Cary Grant (a movie that shows the trials and tribulations of home ownership that was later remade into *The Money Pit* with Tom Hanks) as a Valentine's Day gift.

I had to help my honey open up his great video present since both of his arms were in wrist splints from severe tendonitis caused by all the work he'd been doing on the house.

Missing the bemused expression on his face and not picking up on his nonverbal communication, I cheerfully popped in the video and snuggled in for a fun evening with my sweetie watching Cary Grant and Myrna Loy deal with their first-house difficulties.

We didn't make it even halfway through the video.

I think Michael turned it off about the third time Cary got zinged with another unexpected construction bill.

Maybe it had something to do with all of our unexpected triple-digit hardware bills.

Then there was the Thanksgiving tradition misunderstanding.

Michael's very big on tradition.

He likes to eat the same foods he grew up with on Thanksgiving or Christmas.

So do I—although I'm willing to be a little more adventuresome now and then and add something new to the holiday table.

Not Michael.

At Thanksgiving he's gotta have his turkey, stuffing, mashed potatoes and gravy, pumpkin pie, yams, corn, and creamed peas.

Well, I detest peas—in any way, shape, or form. And there was certainly no way I was going to cream them—yuck!

However, when my sister, Lisa—who doesn't like to

cook—heard that Michael just loved creamed peas, she offered to make them as her Thanksgiving contribution.

But she told me not to say anything to him because she wanted it to be a surprise.

Now Lisa had never made creamed peas before in her life.

Nor had I, and neither of us had a clue as to how to prepare them.

So she looked in cookbook after cookbook before she finally found a recipe.

Turkey Day arrived, and everyone brought their Thanksgiving specialties to our kitchen. Lisa was one of the last to arrive and she came in bearing a clear glass bowl covered in plastic wrap which she proudly removed with a flourish and handed to Michael.

"What's this?" he said, peering down at the milky contents in bewilderment.

"Your favorite," she said. "Creamed peas."

He looked up in surprise to see my mom and me behind Lisa, beaming and smiling at him.

There was an awkward silence for a moment before I hurriedly jumped in and said, "Honey, I told Lisa how creamed peas were a vegetable tradition in your family at Thanksgiving, so she made them special just for you."

"Wow," Michael said. "Thanks, Lisa—that was so sweet of you."

Later, after everyone had gone home, Michael said to me, "Honey, where'd you ever get the idea that I like creamed peas?"

"You told me!" I said.

"No, I didn't."

"Yes, you did."

"Honey, I've never eaten creamed peas in my life," Michael replied.

"Uh-huh—you told me you had them every Thanksgiving."

"You must have misunderstood," he said. "I probably said *green* peas."

"Oh."

But I couldn't tell Lisa. Not after all the hard work she'd gone to.

So for the next three Thanksgivings, Michael ate creamed peas until I finally got up the nerve to admit my mistake to my sister.

Then there's the constant surprise of one of us not telling the other of some events scheduled on the calendar.

This happens to me a lot.

I'll tell Michael of some engagement we have and mark it on the kitchen calendar.

A few days later I'll bring up the engagement, and he has no idea what I'm talking about.

"I told you, honey," I'll patiently explain. "So-and-so invited us over; I told you about it and put it on the calendar."

But he still insists this is the first he's ever heard of it.

"Darling, I remember telling you. Look—it's marked on the calendar and everything."

The problem arises when I go to the calendar to prove my point, and there's nothing written on that date. (I've written it on my office calendar instead.)

Oops.

Michael complains that I hold him responsible for things I *intended* to tell him.

His other complaint is that I wait until he leaves the room to start talking to him about something. By this time, he's clear on the other side of the house and all he can hear is an indistinct mumble.

Hey, can I help it if he's a room sprinter? Just moments before he'd been in my office, so I naturally assume he's right in the next room. How was I supposed to know that my marathon man had already run to the kitchen to get a drink of water?

I guess the key, though, is to concentrate on communication rather than the "failure-to . . ."

Unless, of course, he forgets your anniversary . . . then you can just brain him.

Everyone should be quick to listen, slow to speak.

JAMES 1:19

11

What to Do When Cary Grant Turns Out to Be Mickey Rooney

You open the door with visions of Cary Grant filling your head, and find yourself face-to-face with Mickey Rooney instead.

WHEN YOU'VE BEEN SINGLE for any length of time, friends and family always want to fix you up with someone. "I know the nicest guy. . . ." "You two have so much in common. . . ." Sometimes it works, and occasionally even leads to wedded bliss, but more often than not, fix-ups just fizzle.

I remember I'd gone quite a long stretch without a date and was feeling a bit lonely and undesirable when a newly engaged friend of mine said he'd be happy to fix me up with a friend of his.

Well, I was so desperate I didn't bother to quiz him too much about his friend. All I knew was that he was a Christian and longing for a relationship just about as much as I was.

So what more did I want?

More.

Other than Christianity and singleness, we had absolutely nothing in common.

I loved chocolate. He was allergic to it.

He was a vegetarian. I was a lip-smacking carnivore.

He read strictly nonfiction. I was a die-hard novelholic.

I loved to laugh. He told really bad jokes.

Then we went dancing—in a hotel ballroom full of sixty-something seniors who'd learned to dance with Fred and Ginger. Which was fine with me because I'd always adored their grace and style on the floor. Unfortunately, my date had never heard of Rogers and Astaire, but he had watched *Saturday Night Fever*—one too many times.

However, this fix-up fiasco was tame compared to

one that occurred in my pre-Christian days when I was twenty-two and stationed in England with the air force.

I was riding the train from London to Oxford with a woman I'd recently met—an acquaintance of a friend of a friend.

About midway through our journey, this very sophisticated and attractive woman in her late twenties pulled out an expensive monogrammed compact and began to powder her nose.

I admired the beautiful gold compact, and she told me it was a gift from a "friend."

"Boyfriend?"

"No. Just someone I dated a couple of times."

"Wow! I've never gotten nice presents from any man," I said enviously.

"You're obviously dating the wrong men," she said to me in that wonderful upper-crust English accent. "If you like, I could set you up with someone."

"Twist my arm."

"Do you mind if he's a little older?" she asked. "I know a gentleman in London who's an antiques dealer."

Older-schmolder. Who cares?

Besides, Cary Grant, the epitome of debonair sophistication, was an older man, and I'd date him in a heartbeat. So I eagerly agreed to this fix-up as visions of Cary filled my head.

However, when I opened the door to my date's knock a week later, there stood a florid-faced Mickey Rooney-type instead. (In high heels, I was nearly a foot taller than him.)

But I quickly told myself not to let his height—or lack thereof—stand in my way. After all, he was older (by nearly thirty years), which meant knowledgeable and interesting; and English, which meant well-bred and refined; and an antiques dealer, which naturally meant cultured and intelligent.

So although his height was a bit of a letdown, I prepared myself for a pleasant evening.

However, once we arrived at the elegant restaurant

I'd chosen, I realized all too soon that my well-bred and refined "gentleman" from London was anything but.

My first clue came when he tried to impress me with his knowledge of the French language.

"Gar-cone, gar-cone," he yelled to the waiter.

It was a speedy downhill slide into the roast beef and Yorkshire pudding after that.

On the drive back to the lovely English cottage where I lived with a girlfriend, I kept up a constant stream of chatter about the "land of the free and the brave" in an attempt to avoid the off-color anecdotes that my ribald raconteur seemed determined to share with me.

When we arrived at my house, I discovered much to my dismay that my roommate had gone out for the evening—leaving me alone with a slightly intoxicated Benny Hill-wannabe.

I started to make small talk, and he made a forward pass that left me no doubt as to his intentions.

After I neatly sidestepped this, he dangled a gold bracelet in front of me and made me an offer he thought I couldn't refuse.

That's when daylight finally began to glimmer.

Now I knew how my train acquaintance got her gold compact.

But wait . . . that's not how it happened in the movies!

When Cary Grant gave a woman a gift, there were no strings attached. (At least, none that I could see on camera. But then again, those were the days when movies still left something to the imagination. And my imagination just never took things that far.)

Which is how I found myself in this sticky—and rather scary—situation. (I was a bit nervous because at the time, the Yorkshire Ripper—the '70s version of England's Jack the Ripper—was still roaming the countryside.)

So when the tipsy antique dealer repeated his request a little more obnoxiously, I did the only thing any self-respecting woman interested in saving her skin—and her virtue—would do.

I lied.

"Excuse me, but I have to check in with the base," I told my would-be paramour. "There's a rumor we might be going on alert (war games) tonight, and I may need to report for duty."

I dialed the base—all the while keeping my finger pressed down on the "flash" button—and carried on an animated one-way conversation.

After loudly replacing the receiver, I pasted a chagrined look on my face and returned to my waiting date. "Well, that's the life of a soldier," I said. "I'm sorry, but I'm going to have to cut our evening short. I need to change into my alert gear and report to the base immediately."

"'Cor, I'd love to see you in uniform," he said.

Gosh, didn't this guy ever give up?

I raced upstairs—firmly locking my bedroom door behind me—and quickly changed into my green fatigues and war gear.

"Right, then, I'm ready to go," I said in a muffled voice as I descended the stairs.

His eyes started at the steel-toes of my combat boots, traveled up my baggy fatigues and bulky green field jacket, until finally coming to rest on my gas-masked face and helmeted head.

No way was I going to find myself caught in a lip lock with this London Lothario.

As my Cary-disappointment followed me out to my car, I extended my hand and thanked him for a "lovely" evening while all the time perspiring profusely inside my tightly sealed, kiss-proof protective gas mask.

He waited until I got in my car and began driving away before he turned on his ignition. I kept a careful watch in my rearview mirror as he followed me down the road—until he turned in the opposite direction and headed toward the train station.

Quickly, I pulled down the nearest country lane, shut off my engine, and waited fifteen minutes, until I was sure he was really gone. Then I stealthily made my way back home and crept back into the house—still in full combat regalia.

If any of my English neighbors had been watching, they might well have thought the Battle of Britain was upon them again.

And the moral of the story?

Beware of strangers on a train. Or beware of Brits bearing gifts.

Neither shalt thou covet thy neighbor's house, his field, or his manservant... his ox... or [gold compact].

DEUTERONOMY 5:21 (KJV)

12

"Must You Make That Noise?"

Running for cover when the PMS monster strikes!

HUSBANDS WHO VALUE THEIR LIVES—and their relationship with their wives—know that they might occasionally need to take some evasive action from the dreaded PMS monster.

Many women suffer from PMS (premenstrual syndrome), that oh-so-fun feminine malady that strikes once a month, causing husbands and children to run for cover until the hormonal hurricane has passed.

I have PMS problems too. Except that mine are very specific.

So specific, in fact, that I've even come up with my own word for them: PMSNI (pronounced "pimsnee"—premenstrual syndrome noise irritation).

I first recognized this "pimsnee" phenomenon about ten years ago, when I was still single.

I'd invited my friend Steve over for brunch, and while I was preparing the omelets, he decided to help out by making the orange juice. He opened up a can of frozen juice, dumped it into a large plastic pitcher, added the obligatory water, and began stirring it with a wooden spoon.

Ba-∂um-bum, ba-∂um-bum, ba-∂um-bum thumped the steady, repetitive thud of the spoon against the plastic sides of the pitcher. *Ba-∂um-bum, ba-∂um-bum, ba-∂um-bum*, until suddenly I couldn't stand it any more.

"MUST you make that noise?" I snarled at Steve, turning on him like some crazed fiend.

There went any possibility of a romantic relationship with that man.

It gets worse.

About a year or so later I was living alone in a cute "mother-in-law" cottage close to the college I attended. The only problem with the cottage was the ancient refrigerator that came with it—not exactly the quietest of appliances.

However, most of the time, I could just tune it out.

Until the night I was up late cramming for finals.

At three A.M. I finally decided to grab a few hours' sleep before my morning class.

V-r-r-r-r, v-r-r-r-r, v-r-r-r-r came the steady, incessant noise from the fridge. *V-r-r-r-r, v-r-r-r-r, v-r-r-r-r* it continued, as I tossed and turned trying to block out the persistent whirring. I buried my head beneath my pillow, clapped my hands over my ears—anything to still that angry, annoying sound.

But nothing worked.

Finally, I jumped out of bed and stumbled into the kitchen. Yanking open the freezer door, I peered into its interior trying to identify the culprit.

Ah . . . there it was: the freezer fan.

In desperation, I ripped off the plastic protective covering that shielded the fan. Suddenly, the noise escalated to what sounded to my pimsnee-challenged ears like a deafening roar. Wildly, I looked around the almost empty freezer for something to still the blaring blades. Finally, my bleary eyes fastened on a shiny object in one corner: the foil-wrapped frozen hamburger patty my mother had sent home with me earlier.

Since my immediate need was to silence that fan any way I could, I grabbed the rock-hard patty without thinking and wedged it in between the blades. ("Chick logic" at its finest. Check out my book *Dated Jekyll, Married Hyde* for more "chick logic.")

Ah . . . blessed relief. No more whirring.

Confident of my victory over the G.E. giant, I sleepily staggered back to my welcoming bed. Within moments of my head hitting the pillow, however, my PMS-radar ears picked up a steady, humming sound.

H-u-u-u-m-m-m, h-u-u-u-m-m-m, h-u-u-u-m-m-m the same appliance mocked me with its dastardly droning. Once again, I tried the bury-my-head-beneath-the-pillow trick, but in the absolute stillness of the predawn hours, the hum resounded like crashing cymbals to my tender eardrums.

Discarding my useless pillow, and throwing back the covers, I leapt from the bed—stubbing my toe in the process—and limped to the kitchen where I angrily pulled the plug on the noisy enamel monster.

Now at last I could get some sleep.

Dream on.

This time, as I was about to drift off into never-never land, my acute dog-hearing identified a whoosh of air.

Could it be the wind?

No. One glance out my window showed no trees swaying in the breeze—just the stillness of an early California morning.

Whoosh-whoosh. There it was again.

Where could it be coming from?

As I wandered through the house with bloodhound ears at attention, I realized the sound intensified in the dining room. Like that childhood game of hide-and-seek, I knew that I was getting warmer as I approached the wall heater.

But the heater wasn't even on.

Baffled, I dropped to my knees to investigate.

Eureka! At last I'd located the clamorous culprit.

My ravaged ears begged me to blow out the noisy flickering pilot light keeping me awake, but as much as I longed for a full night's sleep, I wasn't quite ready for a full life's sleep.

Instead, I mustered all the ingenuity I could at four in the morning and hung a thick army blanket across the doorway, wadded cotton balls in my ears, and barricaded myself under every pillow in the house.

At last I slept. Actually, I overslept.

I woke up just seven minutes before my final, and the college was four minutes away. Hurriedly I threw on some sweats, grabbed my backpack, and raced to the car.

Three hours later, when I returned home brain-dead and starving, I was greeted at the door by the smell of rotting meat.

My freezer was never the same again. Just another casualty in the pimsnee war.

My husband-to-be was also another casualty in that ongoing battle.

But he bore his wounds bravely.

The first time he suffered a hormonal hit was one night early in our dating relationship. I've forgotten the particulars of the evening, except that he was driving on a curvy California road somewhere and had a tendency to hug the center line, thereby rolling over all those aggravating little safety-conscious raised road markers.

Ba-dum-bum, ba-dum-bum, ba-dum-bum. It was the same repetitive noise as the orange juice pitcher incident that made me climb out of my skin.

The first couple of times it happened, I let it slide.

After all, he was pretty cute, and I was enjoying looking at his bearded profile. But cute or not, the third time he *ba-dum-bumped* over those center dividers, I lost it.

"MUST you make that noise?" I screeched, clapping my hands over my ears.

Michael was momentarily taken aback, but quickly recovered once I explained my repetitive noise neurosis. (Luckily for me, he'd grown up in a household with four women, so knew firsthand the vagaries of female hormones.)

Recently, I was happy to discover that I'm not the only one with pimsnee problems.

Lana said that her husband's noisy chewing drives her up the wall.

"Oh, does he chew with his mouth open?" I asked sympathetically.

"No. He just chews loudly," she complained. (Although, for some strange reason, she only seems to notice it once a month or so.)

My pimsnee irritation has rubbed off on my husband now, too. Only his would be called TMSNI (Testosterone male syndrome noise irritation, or "timsnee.")

The odd thing is, his noise irritation only seems to kick in at night after I've gone to sleep.

So I snore a little every now and then.

I don't see what the big deal is. It never keeps me awake.

I will watch my ways and keep my tongue from sin; I will put a muzzle on my mouth.

PSALM 39:1

100

13

"I Do, No, I Do Not (Like Your Hobbies)!"

What happens when those wedding-day promises come face-to-face with reality. Before you were married, he enjoyed going shopping; now his idea of a fun date is going to monster truck rallies!

THE "S" WORD STRIKES TERROR in the hearts of many husbands who would rather do just about anything—than shop.

Now, they don't mind grocery shopping too much, because, after all, they have a stake in what kind of meat and potatoes their wives bring home.

But clothes shopping sends most men into a tailspin. And craft fairs? Forget it.

One time my Aunt Sharon tricked my Uncle Jim into going to the marketplace with her.

He thinks they're going grocery shopping, but it turns out "The Marketplace" is a series of craft shops and boutiques in Racine, Wisconsin.

"Boutique": another thing most men hate.

"Since we've been married, I've come to fear any event with the word 'boutique' in it," says Joe Bentz.

"As a single man, I had no idea how many of these things there were, and my wife loves them!

"For me, if you've seen one, you've seen them all. How many things can you possibly make with old coat hangers, balls of cotton, pipe cleaners, and tin cans?

"How many times can you ooh and ahh over little embroidered sayings like World's Greatest Grandma?

"Walking through these things time and time again is agony for many men," Joe says.

Just as hunting and fishing are agony for many women.

For instance, Lisa grew up on a farm, so her husband, Hank, thought she was the outdoorsy type.

"I am, to a certain extent," Lisa said, "but there's no way I could shoot Bambi."

Neither could my Aunt Sharon.

She's been married to Uncle Jim for more than thirty years.

And for more than thirty years, Uncle Jim has gone hunting every Thanksgiving during deer season.

The first year they were married, Jim invited his bride to go along as the cook and bottle washer—to have the meal ready for all the men when they came out of the woods.

Aunt Sharon politely said, "I don't think so."

But she wasn't interested in hunting, either.

"The only kind of shooting I want to do is with a camera."

In the early days of their marriage, Sharon said she used to complain every time Jim went hunting—because she was left alone watching the kids.

But she quickly learned the one thing to take the sting out of this "aloneness."

Shopping.

Uncle Jim, hunting in the woods with his brothers, would say at the end of each day, "Well, there went another thousand dollars."

Later on, as her sons got older and joined their dad on his yearly hunting trips, Sharon would occasionally hop a plane and come visit us out West for a few days.

Although I know she missed us and really wanted to see her California relatives, I think the added attraction was new stores to shop in.

My sister-in-law's husband—also named Jim—is a hunter too.

But he loves to hunt for pheasant. And his tender-hearted wife can never eat what her husband brings home. She'll take one look at the pheasant and say, "the poor bird," and start crying.

Jim also loves sprint car racing.

And his wife, Sheri, will go along to the races with him even though she hates seeing the cars crash.

"Jim loves the Silver Crown races," Sheri said. "I love being with him, so I go."

But since turnabout is fair play, Jim will take her out for coffee, or to nice bed-and-breakfasts—even attend cultural events with her.

However, the last time they went to a musical (my favorite: *Les Misérables*), Jim fell asleep.

That happened to one of my girlfriends too. (Whose name I've agreed not to mention.) Only her husband fell asleep in their very expensive seats at the San Francisco production of *Phantom of the Opera*.

It's difficult for me to understand how anyone can fall asleep at a musical extravaganza.

But then again, most men I know don't understand how I could fall asleep at a major league baseball game.

The Oakland A's, no less.

Several years ago when I was working at a Sacramento newspaper, I managed to scrounge some passes to an A's game from the sports editor—as a birthday gift for my teenage nephew, Josh.

It was Josh's first professional baseball game, so he was in sports heaven.

However, it was a warm, sunny day and nothing much was happening on the ball field. . . .

So, I fell asleep.

Josh couldn't believe it.

"How can you fall asleep at a baseball game, Aunt Laura?" he asked incredulously.

"Well, to be honest, this is pretty boring," I said. "Where's all the home runs?" (Every baseball movie I've ever watched always had at least one spectacular home run, if not more—like *Pride of the Yankees* with Gary Cooper as the great Lou Gehrig.)

But as far as I could tell, at this Oakland game the players just kept walking around the bases.

And for this they get paid more than a million dollars?

I don't get it.

Then again, Jim and my girlfriend's jock husband don't get musicals, either.

At least they don't have a yard full of old cars.

One friend said that a lot of her girlfriends' husbands would buy old cars they planned to fix up.

They'd start to tinker with them, then get diverted by other things—work, family—and the cars wound up as a permanent, and unattractive, part of the landscape.

One husband who wasn't a car buff decided he wanted to install a pool in his backyard—all by himself.

So he cleared some space, dug a hole, then got distracted.

For ten years.

Until, finally, county regulations forced him to finish his swimming pool.

Which was a good thing, since the other wives had threatened to dump their husband's old cars into the unfinished hole in the ground.

After they got home from shopping.

Submit to one another out of reverence for Christ.

EPHESIANS 5:21

14

"You're How Old, and You Still Live With Your Mother?"

Guys (and gals) speak out on what drives
them crazy on a date.

1. Boy, I'm hungry. I hope you brought enough money.
2. I think our children will be good-looking.
3. You remind me of my ex.
4. My wife is out of town.
5. Can I order the whole right side of the menu?
6. Now, we're second cousins, not first . . . right?
7. Do you color your hair?
8. What's your gross annual income?
9. My alimony check is late.
10. You're *how* old, and you still live with your mother?

Now and then the sexes can drive each other crazy.

The list above—drawn from an informal survey I conducted among singles ranging in age from twenty-five to sixty-five—is just a sampling of some of the things we say to the opposite sex that makes them nuts.

For instance, a male chiropractor I know said that when he moved to California from the Midwest every woman he met would ask, "What do you do?"

Once they learned he was a chiropractor, their eyes turned green—with dollar signs.

"Oh . . . how long have you been in practice?" they'd ask. "Do you have a lot of clients?" "What part of town is your office in?"

Another guy told me that he and a woman friend had gone out to dinner—he didn't think they were dating—and the meal was supposed to be Dutch treat. But after dinner, the woman said to him, "Oh, why don't you be a man and pay for the whole thing?"

He said he didn't realize his masculinity was tied to his wallet.

Then there's my girlfriend who went out on a blind date with a guy and he said, rather hesitantly, "Do you remember when you asked me if I had a roommate?"

Something clicked and she said, "You're married."

He said "Yup."

She said, "Take me home."

Mark, a twenty-seven-year-old lawyer originally from Texas, says his big beef with women is: "Tell me what you're thinking!"

"The whole 'mind reader' thing really bugs me," he said. "I wish they'd just tell me what they're thinking, 'cause I can't figure it out."

You're not alone, Mark.

But take heart. Once you've been married a few years, you'll know what she's thinking.

Or not.

Personally, after being single—and confused about the whole dating/singles group scene—for so many years, I finally got to the point where I just came out and said what was on my mind.

That's why the first time I went out with Michael, I blurted, "Is this a date?"

I didn't want any misunderstandings or false expectations—having had more than my fair share of them with the dozens of male "buddies" from my singles group. So I thought I'd just clear the air right up front.

My forthrightness worked for us—we're now married.

But it doesn't have the same effect on all men.

Take a male single friend of ours in his early forties who's having a nice, pleasant dinner with a woman friend.

"Suddenly the subject of marriage comes up," says our fortyish friend, "and she says, 'Well, what about you? How do you feel about getting married someday?'"

Can you say, "uncomfortable"?

Romance is the last thing on his mind, and now out

of the blue his friend has brought up the "M" word.

He usually skips dessert.

The "D" word—dating—is also a difficult area in this day and age for some guys.

For instance, my friend Harley says that a lot of women in their thirties and forties in his church singles group complain that "the men at this church don't date."

"Well, there's nothing to stop you from picking up the phone," he'll retort.

Harley, who is forty-three and content in his singleness—at this time in his life—believes that once men and women get to be in their thirties and forties, the "rules" about a woman not calling a man or making the first move no longer apply.

"It's an even playing field," he said.

"I think a single woman calling up and asking a guy over for dinner is nice," Harley said, adding that it's often a good way to begin a friendship.

And friendship sometimes turns into a "relationship."

But none of the friendships I had ever did.

Of course, I was in a singles group where the guys didn't date, either.

And, I was old-fashioned enough to want the guy to make the move—after about one hundred moves on my part that never got me anywhere—so that I'd know for certain he was interested in me romantically.

This confused Michael a bit when we first met and were sitting at the same table along with some other friends during a church potluck and talent show.

After the show, Michael got up to go visit some friends at another table. I wanted to hang around and talk to him some more, but my girlfriends propelled me from the room, saying, "If he's interested, he'll make a move. Don't be so available."

Well, he did make a move, but after we got together he also told me that at first he didn't think *I* was interested because I left so abruptly.

Then there are the men who are very interested, and making moves too, but the woman doesn't respond.

Mark tells the story of a girl he dated off and on for a few months in college.

"I had the biggest crush on her," he said, "but she'd never call me back or want to do anything when I called. So finally I got the hint and said, 'Fine, I'm not going to call anymore.'"

A couple of months passed and Mark was in the middle of studying for exams. On his way home from the library, he spotted a note on his car. "Hey, I've missed you and hanging out with you," his former crush had written on the back of a deposit slip.

So, he expectantly looks her up, and she tells him she's just gotten engaged.

Oh, the games people play.

Then there's my niece, Letitia, a young dater-in-training who always wanted her boyfriend to take her out to a nice candlelight dinner.

His idea of a nice restaurant, however, was Jacques in ze Box.

But I told her not to be dismayed; she's only eighteen, she's got plenty of time.

Singleness can be fraught with confusion and contradiction.

Michael recalls the time he was attending a church where the pastor addressed all the single men from the pulpit, saying: "Are you coming here to worship God, or are you coming here to meet women?"

"Are the two mutually exclusive?" Michael asked. "Should I come to church to worship God and go to bars to meet women?"

Still another man wondered why women have a problem if a man lives with his mother.

"Perhaps he's just being a good son and taking care of her," he said. "What's wrong with that?"

Nothing.

As long as the guy doesn't bring Mom along on his dates.

For this reason a man will leave
his father and mother.

GENESIS 2:24

15

Time to Go: Ready or Not

*You're planning to go somewhere and you say,
"I'm ready." He heads for the door;
keys in hand. Ten minutes later he finds
you in the bathroom brushing your teeth.
(Your were just "ready" to start "getting ready.")*

MEN AND WOMEN tell time differently.

Ask any husband.

For instance, a couple plans to go somewhere, and she'll say, "I'm ready." He grabs the keys and heads for the door.

But she's not ready.

She's just ready to *start* getting ready. Ten minutes later she's still in the bathroom.

Meanwhile, getting antsy, her husband leaves his post at the front door to tinker with something.

When she finally emerges from putting the finishing touches on her hair and makeup, she notices her husband busy doing something, so decides to just "straighten up a bit" while she waits for him.

I speak from firsthand experience.

I admit I'm not the best judge of time, but given that numbers are involved, you'd think Michael would be a little more understanding since he knows I'm math-challenged.

The reality is, I'm just trying to be considerate of my husband.

After all, once I've finished getting ready and notice that he's out puttering in the garden or working in the garage, I naturally don't want to interrupt—that would be rude.

Instead, I find something to do to occupy myself until *he's* ready.

Meanwhile, he's outside being productive, thinking he's waiting for me.

When he finally finishes whatever it is he's doing and comes inside to see me straightening up the kitchen, he

115

gets frustrated and says, "C'mon, honey. We're going to be late!"

"I'm ready," I'll say innocently. "I'm just waiting for you."

I don't understand why this bugs him so much.

"Jill" can relate.

"I'm dressed, ready to go, so my husband gets ready," she says.

"He's ready, opening the door thinking I'm right behind him—because I'm 'ready,' right?—and I'm elsewhere to be found—putting dishes away, cleaning up the kitchen, applying last-minute touches to my makeup.

"*Now* when I say I'm ready, my husband doesn't move from his chair, knowing full well that it's just a five-minute warning till I'm really ready."

Her husband has figured out that she's really and truly ready once she's standing at the door saying, "Ready to go?"

It's flip-flopped in our marriage.

Our problem begins in the shower.

I take a five-minute shower and need about twenty minutes afterward to get ready, while Michael takes twenty-minute showers and only needs five minutes to get ready.

Therefore, Michael logically thinks that if I shower first, then I have twenty minutes to get ready while he's showering.

And once he gets out and dresses, we'll both be ready to go.

It doesn't work that way.

That's because I'm in my own time zone.

While he's showering, I spend those twenty minutes doing other things around the house—checking my e-mail, unloading the dishwasher, etc.

Once I hear the shower stop, I know that I now have twenty minutes to get ready.

Naturally, Michael always finishes getting ready before me, and has to wait.

Once I'm finished and on my way to the door, I can't

find Michael, so I call out impatiently, "C'mon, honey, we've got to get going or we'll be late!"

Good thing those marriage vows say "for better or for worse."

Katie and Mark live in the country, where everything takes a little longer. For instance, if they run out of milk, it's not just a quick run down the street to the convenience store—it's a good half hour to the nearest grocery store.

So they have to plan their time very carefully.

When they're getting ready for a trip into town, Mark will say to Katie, "Okay, you're ready?"

"I'm ready," she'll answer.

So Mark goes out to warm up the pickup truck before meeting Katie at the door—where he usually winds up waiting for her anywhere from five to ten minutes—with truck idling.

Recently, having just filled up the truck with a full tank of gas, Mark said to Katie on his way out the door, "Try to make it out before I run out of gas."

Other husbands who have been married many years have just resigned themselves to the wait.

My friend Lisa said that after eighteen years of waiting, her husband Hank has given up on her.

"He just watches TV until I get there," she says.

In some marriages, however, it's the husband who's got the time impairment.

Take Bill and Annie.

Annie's learned to start saying, "Dinner's on" about five minutes before it actually is because it takes Bill so long to get to the table.

"Bill caught on, however, and figured when I said, 'Dinner's on,' he still had plenty of time.

"I started saying it louder and earlier," she said ruefully. "You can see the progression."

Another woman says it's her *husband* who takes forever to get ready.

"He claims he's just waiting for me to get out of the bathroom before he starts his routine, but half an hour later he's still primping and asking me, 'Does this match?'"

Then there's Quenten and Doris.

"Quenten likes to be early to everything," Doris says. "Preferably half an hour at least.

"I like to be 'on time,' which ranges from five minutes prior to five minutes after—unless, of course, a crowd is expected. Then we both like to be early—Quenten by at least an hour, I by twenty to thirty minutes."

Now, *that* I can't relate to at all.

The last thing I was early to was my wedding. (And that's only because I was getting dressed at the church and my maid of honor drove.)

Now, Debbie is a woman after my own heart.

"I have a problem gauging how much time is necessary for travel, shopping, etc.," she says. "Sometimes when I tell my husband my plans, he'll say, 'You don't have enough time to do all that.'

"He's usually right."

I hate it when that happens.

Especially 'cause it happens to me—a lot.

I'll make up a list of things to do—like go to the drugstore to pick up a prescription, drop off clothes at the dry cleaners, pick up dog food, get my hair trimmed—and plan to be out at my folks' house—a mere twenty-five minutes away—all in the space of one hour.

Invariably, I'm anywhere from fifteen to forty-five minutes late.

Which is why I now build in a two-hour lateness window anytime I'm going out to my folks'.

Another way I've found to beat my time gauge problem is to set every clock in the house to a different time.

Our bedroom alarm clock is half an hour fast—at Michael's insistence, so he has the perceived luxury of sleeping in—the clock on the VCR in the den is five minutes slow (which I keep meaning to change since I always miss the beginning of *Jeopardy*), and the clock in my office is ten minutes fast so I can feel I've accomplished a lot in a short period of time.

The only problem is, I sometimes confuse the VCR clock with my office clock and wind up late anyway.

This time problem isn't peculiar only to married couples either.

For instance, Jared Frederick Budenski, a psychology major at Dakota Wesleyan University, sent me an e-mail about one date he'll never forget.

"This girl and I were planning to go out for a soda and just to hang out, then we were going to go for a walk and watch a video," Jared said. "When I called her to see if she was ready to go, she said come on up."

The problem was, Jared lived only two minutes away from his date, and when he arrived to pick her up, she wasn't quite ready. So her parents intercepted and he spent an awkward fifteen minutes—or an eternity—making small talk with them.

"Finally, she came out ready to go," Jared said. "She had her hair done, perfume on, the whole nine yards, and I just had on a T-shirt and pants."

The two went out for soda and hung out awhile just having fun, then decided to go on their walk. The only problem was, before his date could take a walk, she said she needed to change into athletic clothes.

Which took another fifteen minutes. (More small talk with the folks.)

But Jared says the walk was nice and they had a good conversation, then came back to watch the video.

However, before sitting down in front of the TV, his date said she needed to change, so she took a shower and changed out of her athletic clothes into a nice outfit—which took another thirty minutes.

By that time, Jared said, he could almost have watched the video.

"I guess 'I'm ready' really meant 'give me an extra hour,'" he said.

Just wait till he gets married.

There is a time for everything . . .
a time to search and a time to give up,
a time to keep and a time to throw away.

ECCLESIASTES 3:1, 6

16

A Jekyll/Hyde
Love Story

*Or how a special kind of love changed a prissy,
opinionated snob into a champion of "cute."*

I'VE ALWAYS BEEN what you might call "opinion-ated." Especially in the area of what I like and don't like.

And I'm not shy about expressing myself.

People who know me learn pretty quickly my likes and dislikes.

At the very top of my dislike list is math. Actually, dislike's too mild a word.

I hate math. It gives me a headache.

That's why I'm a writer.

Writers don't do math.

However, while I've been busy trying to earn my living as an author, I've had to take various jobs every now and then to help my hardworking husband pay the bills.

One such job was demonstrating and selling gourmet kitchen products to women in their homes in a party-like atmosphere. Since I love to cook (and eat) I figured it would be a piece of cheesecake.

Wrong.

Math was involved.

I had to tally up people's orders, figure out tax and discount percentages, then go home and transfer all that information to one large order form—and get it to balance.

Balancing was the problem. It's never been my strong suit—even with a calculator.

So the day I spent more than eight and a half hours trying to get fifteen orders to add up correctly, I realized it wasn't my calling, so turned in my calculator and hung up my apron.

Running a close second to math on my list of dislikes is peas. And in rapid succession, the rest of my list includes: rats, mice, and any other type of rodent; football; very hot or very cold weather (below 65 and above 90); turnips, Brussels sprouts, and most nuts (except peanuts, cashews, or chocolate-covered macadamia nuts); horror movies; the colors lime green or orange—especially in articles of clothing; and anything bordering on darling or "cutesy" (including ducks, bunnies, teddy bears, cats, and dogs).

I know I've probably offended more than half my readers with that last statement, but read on.

The "cutesy" part all changed with Gracie.

Gracie is Lady Grace Elizabeth Walker, our beloved American Eskimo—a descendant of the Spitz family—who looks like a little white fox.

Yep. A dog.

Now, I've never been a pet person.

Sure, growing up we had the obligatory goldfish (that died), hamster (that my dad accidentally squashed under our '50s hi-fi speaker), and puppies (which my brothers claimed), but I don't recall bonding with any of them.

I guess that's because I was too busy bonding with my books.

The fantasy world I lived in was so much more exotic and exciting than something so ordinary as a pet.

Then, when I got older, I got a bit "prissy."

That is, if you call having an aversion to the fragrance of kitty litter prissy. Or cat hairs on the sofa or in my soup, when I'd visit my female friends with felines.

I've never understood the cat connection so many of my women friends have.

Or that dog connection, either.

They may be man's best friend, but they've never been mine.

Besides shedding all over the place and leaving little tokens of affection on your best carpet, they've also been known to decimate a coffee table of fragile china teacups with just a couple wags of their happy tails.

But aside from all the peculiar peccadilloes of our

non-human friends, what I really don't get is how so many intelligent, well-educated humans can turn into such goofy, gooey, baby-talking sentimentalists. Over an animal!

Even when she's a dawling, bwootiful widdle pwincess who wuvs her mommy.

Oh no! I've gone over the edge into the cutesy world of baby talk! Now there's no turning back.

I never dreamed it would happen to me.

Sure, I laughed and cried over the antics of James Herriot's animal friends, but never having been a pet owner, I just thought it was more of an England thing and a book thing than an animal thing.

My husband, on the other hand, grew up with dogs and has always adored them.

Which is why finally, during our fifth year of marriage, I relented and said I'd be open to getting a dog.

But not without some stipulations.

"It" couldn't shed, had to be housebroken, and would never, ever, be allowed on our bed.

Well, when we first got Gracie—named after Grace Kelly (not just because of the silvery-blond-hair similarity, but because she's quite the regal little thing)—she was short-haired and mellow.

A perfect addition to our couch potato family.

She simply loved to just lay there and be petted.

She never even barked.

Our first clue that something was amiss came when the vet asked us if she was lethargic.

"No, just very mellow," we said naïvely.

Wrong.

Turned out she had allergies and worms.

Dewormed and on a controlled diet, she now has longer hair than both my husband and I put together.

And it shows up beautifully on our teal green carpet.

But that's okay. My floors look better than they ever did before because I'm vacuuming more frequently now. (And I was under the mistaken impression that having a dog would make my house dirtier.)

Gracie's kicked that lethargy thing too.

She gives new meaning to the word "zoom"—especially when we first let her out into the yard. I think my husband clocked her at one hundred miles per hour. (But that's dog-miles, so it was really only fifty, I think. . . . Whatever. It's a math thing.)

Yet of all the aspects of dog ownership, the thing that amazes me the most is how much Gracie loves me. (She was supposed to be Michael's dog, and she likes him an awful lot. But she's in love with me.)

I always knew dogs were loyal, devoted, and even heroic at times. After all, I grew up with Lassie and Scooby-Doo.

But this adoration stuff came as a complete surprise.

Now, Michael's pretty great in the unconditional love department, but he doesn't paw enthusiastically at the air and cover my hand with wet kisses the minute I walk through the front door.

Well, at least not as often as Gracie.

She follows me everywhere too.

In fact, right now as I'm trying to finish this chapter, she just came up and poked her head up under my elbow, looking for a little affection. I told her I was writing about her, but she wasn't the least bit interested in recognition or fame.

She just wanted some love.

Which I was only too happy to give.

All right, all right, I admit it. I'm head-over-heels, crazy in love with our little Gracie. (Almost sickeningly so, say those who knew me in my pre-dog days.)

In fact, the first time we had to take her to the vet for shots I felt like a criminal.

Gracie stood on her little hind legs, wrapped her paws around my neck, laid her soft white head on my shoulder and clung to me for dear life—shaking all the while.

"Mommy, mommy, don't let them hurt me," her big black eyes begged as the vet gently pulled her away to administer the shot.

I felt like a murderer.

But, thankfully, she forgave me.

She's a very loving dog.

When Michael comes home from work at night and greets me with a hug and a kiss, Gracie jumps right in, wanting a piece of that affection action.

"Group hug," Michael and I will chorus, scooping Gracie up into our arms.

She also sleeps at the bottom of our bed now. (Yes, *on* the bed, but she always waits patiently until we put her blanket on top of our quilt.)

Have I mentioned how smart Gracie is?

She can sit, shake, play dead, say please, dance, and play the piano. (She's not quite ready for "Für Elise," but we both see "Chopsticks" in her future.)

The thing that has surprised Michael the most about my Gracie connection is how some of my earlier adamant opinions about what I like and don't like have changed so drastically.

Big-time Jekyll/Hyde switch.

And he's not quite used to it yet.

For instance, recently we were out shopping, and I saw some of those big, fluffy animal slippers that I used to hate.

"Look honey, aren't they cute?" I crooned. "Maybe I'll get some for Christmas," I hinted. Then we passed by some stuffed animals and I began playing with them.

Now our home boasts a stuffed bunny, duck, reindeer, and two teddy bears. (All toys for Gracie—except for one of the teddy bears, which Michael gave me as a Valentine's present.)

How many are your works, O Lord!
In wisdom you made them all;
the earth is full of your creatures.

PSALM 104:24

17

Aerobics Queen Wrestles the Couch Potato

She works out at the gym three times a week, while he practices finger exercises on the remote control. Can a fitness buff and a slug find true happiness?

WHEN TONI FIRST MET LES, she was a size nine and an aerobics instructor—teaching at least three times a week.

She also rode her bike everywhere since she didn't have a car.

Now, that woman was in shape.

After they started dating, Les, wanting to impress Toni, decided to attend her class.

"He tried to play like it wasn't tough for him," Toni says. "And he held out for the entire class—though later he told me he was dying inside but wouldn't quit, just so he could say he lasted through the whole thing.

"He was trying to show me he was the exercising type."

Toni says that later, after they got married and she had children, she gained a lot of weight.

"Les didn't birth any children, but he, too, gained weight."

That's why the two of them now try to exercise together.

"His exercise is sitting on the couch at night eating cinnamon rolls religiously, while I try to stop eating at six P.M. and maybe take a class or two a week," says Toni.

When they decided to "work out" together, Les wanted it to be on his terms—walking terms, that is.

"Well, I'm five-four and Les is six-two," Toni says. "His fast walk was a literal 'jog' for me. Then he told me I couldn't keep up—my payback for working him so hard in that class back then!"

Toni has since lost a few dress sizes, but Les has

gained a few pants sizes. (He got tired of walking.)

"I'm eating salads and trying to cook healthy," says Toni. "He's buying doughnuts and pastries at work and bringing them home. He even puts cheesecakes and pies in the refrigerator—next to my bottled water.

"I don't know how we're doing it, but we're happy. I wouldn't care if he weighed as much as a truck, I'd still love him to death."

Then there's my brother-in-law, Jim, who after he gets off work settles into the sofa as the original couch potato.

He'd be happy watching TV twenty-four hours a day—as long as it's golf, football, or anything sports related.

The one exercise he'll leave the couch for, however, is the driving range.

His wife will occasionally watch a video—from the vantage point of her exercise bike. But she much prefers a walk around her neighborhood instead, with a book on tape.

I like to walk too.

Just don't ask me to run.

I have another friend—Pat from Sebastopol—who feels the same way.

Only she married a runner. In fact, her husband ran the L.A. marathon.

And Pat supported him in his endeavor. She watched it on TV.

However, she says she did participate in some of the training.

In preparation for the marathon, the runners had to "carb up" on a pasta dinner.

Pat carbed up right along with them.

Running and exercising just isn't her forte. (I know how she feels.)

As does an editor friend of mine who shared his theory of exercise with me: "God gave us a finite number of heartbeats ... and when you exercise, you use them

up faster! Thus, couch potatoes have a leg up on im-
mortality."

Pat's friends don't share this view. In fact, one of her
girlfriends is an active mountain climber who recently
climbed Mount Rainier on her vacation.

But before tackling the challenging mountain, her
friend worked out for weeks.

Pat said she couldn't understand working out so you
can go on vacation.

Me either. But then again, I don't get working out in
general.

My favorite workout is hitting the mute button on the
remote control during commercials, while ambidex-
trously turning the pages of my favorite mystery. Or rap-
idly reading two books one after the other in my bubble
bath.

I have been known to break a sweat now and then,
however.

On one of our camping trips, I hiked the entire trail.

Okay, so it was only 1.2 miles. And, okay, so it was
wheelchair accessible. I still hiked it!

I wasn't always such a couch potato.

In fact, in my grade school days, I was quite the
skinny tomboy—often outrunning and outbicycling most
of the boys in my class.

But for some reason that changed in high school—
hormones, maybe?

These days my preferred forms of exercise are walking the dog around the block and finger aerobics.

I type 100 words a minute.

Until recently, I didn't even own an up-to-date pair
of athletic shoes. (I'm so far behind the sports times, I
was still calling them "tennies.") But Michael insisted
that I get a good pair of "athletic" shoes—even for just
walking the dog—so I let him drag me to a sporting
goods store to try on shoes.

I felt like a stranger in a strange land.

There were running shoes, walking shoes, skipping
shoes, shoes for tennis, shoes for basketball, shoes for

soccer, even shoes for surfing. In fact, there were specialized shoes for every activity known to man—except reading.

I tried on a couple pairs and felt like an astronaut walking on the moon in those ungainly space boots.

Well, perhaps I exaggerate a little.

It was really more like putting on those big clunky ski boots and trying to walk in them. Believe it or not, I know whereof I speak. I've actually skied twice in my life—even once in the Swiss Alps—although, technically, the ski instructor called what I did "snowplowing."

Whatever.

The ski lodge was great—that Swiss hot chocolate is out of this world—and I made sure I sent everyone I knew a postcard saying, "Skiing in the Alps this weekend—wish you were here."

Some people just aren't athletic. And I'm one of them.

Which my ex-boyfriend found out early in our dating days.

He'd asked me to go rafting and I told him I wasn't much into water sports, but he assured me that this was just going to be a lazy summer afternoon gently gliding down the river.

And that I wouldn't even get wet.

Taking him at his word, I dressed accordingly, and headed out with him and our friends for a day of fun in the summer sun.

My rude awakening came early in the day when we had to launch our rafts by wading into the river—on foot!

My tennis shoes (they weren't athletic shoes yet) got soaked. And so did the hem of my shorts.

"You said I wouldn't get wet," I wailed.

That was his first clue that our relationship wasn't going to work.

It wasn't that I was prissy or worried about breaking a nail or anything. (I bite my nails, after all.)

It's just that going on the information he had given

me, I wasn't expecting to get wet, so it was kind of a soggy surprise.

Although I should have realized that our rafting experience would be a bust since it involved water.

I've always been kind of afraid of the water—owing to a traumatic incident as a child—when I dived into the pool at the local YWCA and hit my head on the bottom.

I was telling Michael of this childhood trauma over at my parents' house one night when my mom suddenly interrupted and said, "Laura, that was *me. You* didn't ever hit your head on the bottom of the pool—*I* did."

Maybe that's my problem.

My aversion to anything aerobic stems from all the people in my life—or on TV—who got hurt on the sports battlefield.

I've assimilated their pain and trauma as my own.

Maybe that's why ever since the summer of the 1996 Olympics my ankle's been hurting something fierce.

> *Go to the ant, you sluggard;*
> *consider its ways and be wise!*

PROVERBS 6:6

18

More Honeymoon
Horror Stories

True tales of honeymoon mishaps.

THE DAY BEFORE their outdoor wedding, a hurricane passed through town.

But the wedding day dawned clear and beautiful, and the ceremony went off without a hitch.

Unfortunately, the same cannot be said of their honeymoon.

My brother Dave and his wife, Elisa, will probably go down in history as the couple with the most disastrous honeymoon ever.

The debacle began on their wedding night when Dave got sick to his stomach. Rather than indulging in the romantic evening they'd planned, they watched *Star Trek* instead. (Now, if it were Picard and Riker, that would be one thing. But it was still Kirk and Spock.)

Dave was so sick for the next four days they had to reshuffle their reservations at some charming bed-and-breakfasts up and down Cape Cod.

Finally, he started feeling better, so they went to pick up their rental car. However, instead of the compact economy car they'd requested, the only available vehicles were a Lincoln town car or a midsize sedan.

Settling for the sedan, they were finally off on their honeymoon—driving up the Connecticut Turnpike.

The first clue that something was wrong came when they pulled off for a pit stop and the passenger door wouldn't open.

Elisa had to clamber out through the driver's side.

As twilight descended, auto problem number two arose.

Headlights. Only the high beams worked.

Ever resourceful, Dave pulled over and unplugged one set of headlights—burning himself in the process.

Realizing by now that they'd never make it to their darling bed-and-breakfast, they spent the night in a tacky motel next to the interstate.

The next morning, Dave called the rental company about their defective car, and they told him he could either drive back to where he'd rented it and trade it in for the Lincoln, or they could move on to the next rental site two hours away at an airport.

Wanting to move forward with the honeymoon, they opted for the airport site.

Once they arrived, though, no car had been reserved for them. All that was available was another Lincoln town car and a Renault Alliance—with a possible bad starter.

Not wanting a gas guzzler, Dave decided to test the Renault. It started right up.

And they started a brand-new day of the blissful honeymoon they'd envisioned.

They thought.

They took a quick day trip to Provincetown, parked their car in an all-day parking lot, and spent a fun day shopping and visiting art galleries.

At the end of the evening, when they returned to the car, it wouldn't start.

So my brother crawled underneath it and tried to cross the starter wire with a metal spoon from their picnic basket.

No such luck.

And the car was in a no-overnight-parking zone.

Dave and Elisa walked to a nearby restaurant to call a taxi, but discovered to their dismay that there was no taxi service after midnight.

Meanwhile, a local policeman walked in to find out what was the problem.

Upon hearing their sad tale, he kindly offered to drive them back to the last town, whereupon he would hand them off to the police there who would then drive them to the town before that and hand them off to the next policeman—using the cops up and down the Cape as a shuttle service between municipalities—until they returned my brother and his wife to their starting point.

Dave and Elisa were touched by the kind offer, but the officer cautioned them that if a call came in during the shuttling, they'd have to drop them off on the side of the road.

They thanked the man in blue, but started scouting out nearby accommodations that were still open.

Turned out the only vacancy in town was a room to rent in a bar.

They grabbed it.

Once upstairs, however, they were greeted by a crooked floor and sheer window curtains, which offered no protection from the neon sign flashing onto the floorboards.

And only one light bulb—in the bathroom.

"None of the other lights were working," Dave said. "The nightstands had lamps on them, but the bulbs didn't come on, so I checked and there were no bulbs in the lamps. We wondered just what they did with them...." (And they thought the first place was tacky.)

Elisa spent that night of her dream honeymoon crying herself to sleep.

Bright and early the next morning, my brother called the car rental agency in Massachusetts to complain.

They transferred his call to a customer service employee in Texas.

By this time, Dave was so angry he said he didn't want another one of their cars—although it turns out there were none available anyway—and insisted that they rent him an automobile from a different rental agency—since they'd failed so miserably with the first two cars.

After seven minutes on hold, the customer service rep returned and said their original agent had just voided their contract.

They were now on their own.

So there they were, stuck in a coffee shop in Provincetown, Massachusetts, with no transportation and still trying to begin their honeymoon.

Dave called the airport rental agency, but they had no vehicles available, either. Frustrated, he finally took a taxi to the airport and just sat at the car rental counter until the agent could find him anything drivable.

They said they'll never forget their "honeymoon from hell."

But all was not lost.

Two years later they had the opportunity to go to Hawaii on

vacation, so they decided to call that their honeymoon instead.

My in-laws, Jim and Sheri, also had a delayed honeymoon, due to work constraints.

By the time they were finally able to schedule time away for a trip to Disneyland, they'd already been married six months. Over shrimp Creole at The Pirates of the Caribbean—which Sheri didn't have the stomach for—she told Jim that she thought she was pregnant.

Talk about a honeymoon surprise!

Then there's Deirdre and her husband, Jonathan, who had a dream honeymoon in the Bahamas.

"An island band drummed a calypso beat while my new husband and I relaxed together on the floating deck," said Deirdre. "He was playing with his five-day-old wedding ring. Sliding it off and on, bridging his forefingers and rolling it from one hand to another, twirling it on his pinkies . . .

"Suddenly, I heard 'Ting, ting, ting,' and out of the corner of my eye saw something small and sparkly roll across the deck. Seemingly picking up speed, it bounced and careened over splinters and spaces, teetered along twelve to eighteen inches on the edge of a plank—neither of us could move fast enough—when finally, in one very aerobic move, my husband swooped down and snatched it up.

"I've never seen him play with his ring since."

At least that island honeymoon was better than the one where the groom got stung by a jellyfish through the front of his swimming trunks.

Do not boast about tomorrow, for you do not know
what a day may bring forth.

PROVERBS 27:1

19

Gidget Meets Monty Python

Or the battle of the no-brainers.

RECENTLY I SAT DOWN to watch one of my husband's favorite movies with him—a movie I'd never seen: *Monty Python and the Holy Grail*. He'd been telling me about it for years—how funny it was—and reciting whole sections of dialogue from memory. Finally I decided I just had to see what the big deal was.

I fell asleep. Twice. On consecutive nights.

And didn't laugh at all. (Well, maybe once—which is one more time than I laughed at any of the other no-brainer comedies he generally prefers. But that's probably because it was an English movie and just about anything with an English accent works for me.) My husband—and many men I know—just loves those goofy no-brainers complete with puns and pratfalls.

And I don't get it.

But then again, I don't get "The Far Side" either. Michael usually has to explain it to me.

I'm just not a joke person.

In fact, the only joke I can ever remember is one I learned in the second grade: "What does the Pink Panther say when he steps on an insect?"

"Dead ant. Dead ant . . ." (Sung to the tune of "The Theme From the Pink Panther.")

However, I think I'm going to have to come up with a new one soon because even my five-year-old nephew Dylan knows that joke.

Michael and I just have different tastes in some areas. For instance, on Friday nights after a long, hard week at work, we're usually both in the mood for a good no-brainer movie. The problem is, his no-brainers and my no-brainers are not even remotely on the same brainwave.

He wants *Ernest Goes to Camp* or *Ace Ventura, Pet Detective*, while I'm partial to *Gidget Goes Hawaiian*.

I just don't understand how he can like those silly slapstick movies.

But he doesn't understand why I care if Gidget and Moondoggie ever get back together (or why they even broke up in the first place).

That's easy. It's a relationship thing.

It's also a nostalgic thing.

Gidget was part of my childhood. As were *Tammy, Where the Boys Are*, and all those summer beach movies with Frankie and Annette.

Michael thinks they're all pretty stupid.

But then, I think all those movies with exploding chickens, impossibly-contorted faces, and silly puns are pretty dumb.

I just don't get it.

But then, Michael doesn't understand how I was once hooked on soap operas either.

Hey, what can I say? It was another one of those relationship things.

Besides, I was hospital-bound at the time and it became a welcome diversion to see if Erica and Dimitri would ever get together. (For those of you who don't know, they did. But then they broke up a few months later. And last I heard, they were considering a third trip down the aisle.) Oops. My sources say they just broke up again and Dimitri married someone else.

I can't understand why Michael never got into soap operas.

Probably because he's never been much of a TV person (other than *Jeopardy* and *Home Improvement*—which we both love).

He is a movie person, however.

So am I.

We both love the old black-and-white classics, all those glorious MGM musicals, and anything Disney, of course—the old Disney.

Additionally, Michael used to work for a video dis-

146

tributor, and part of his job was to preview movies for his customers before they were sent to video stores.

And they paid him to do this.

I was only too happy to help him out with this difficult aspect of his job when we first got married. However, what I didn't realize was that he had to watch all kinds of movies: the good, the bad, and the awful. When he brought home kick-boxing videos or no-brainer comedies, I'd suddenly remember a friend I had to visit, or some homework I had to do.

Oh, maybe that's what happened. His brain got fried from movie overload and he could no longer tell the difference between funny and silly.

But how does that explain the rest of the men in the world?

And their preference for The Three Stooges?

Women don't get The Three Stooges. Just what is it about them that's so funny, anyway?

They make strange noises and that Moe guy is always so mean—twisting Larry and Curley's ears, or poking them in the eyes, or slapping them in the face.

It's so violent.

That's why I don't like boxing or football, either.

I do, however, like relationship films and period English pieces. (Or in the more common vernacular, "chick flicks.")

Michael will watch them with me every once in a while.

But when more than half an hour passes and everyone's still just sitting around talking, he's outta there.

I guess it's all a matter of taste.

Which extends to Christmas movies as well.

We all have our favorites: *Miracle on 34th Street, White Christmas,* etc.

But while one of my friends likes to watch *It's a Wonderful Life,* every Christmas, her husband prefers one of those action/adventure films released during the holiday season. (To him, they fall into the Christmas movie category because there's usually a shot of a Christmas tree in one of the buildings that gets blown up.)

It's a guy thing.

Most guys really love their action/adventure movies. Why?

The "noise factor."

"Guys like noise," Mike from our Bible study explained to me.

A typical "chick flick" has people sitting around talking and relating—which is what most women enjoy, whereas a typical guy movie has lots of sound: tires screeching, buildings blowing up, scary monsters crashing through a village—more of a "doing" or "action" kind of thing. (Oh, now I get why they like The Three Stooges! It's the noise thing.)

Michael was pleasantly surprised, however, to discover that I can enjoy a good action film with the best of them. With the emphasis on "good." (Which to me translates as anything with Mel Gibson or Harrison Ford.)

However, when the action includes pratfalls, people's eyes bugging out, and bad puns, I just pick up a good mystery and my Calgon and head for the tub.

And Michael takes Gracie for a long walk when I turn on *Gidget*.

That's why now on Friday nights we watch classics like *Arsenic and Old Lace*, *Bringing Up Baby*, or *Jurassic Park*. (Although the noise factor in the latter definitely qualifies it as a guy movie, the relationship between the male and female scientists—and the kids—gives me that chick-flick element I crave, so we're both happy.)

Besides, we did promise to love each other through "better or worse" and that applies to movie tastes as well!

*Let your eyes look straight ahead, fix your gaze
directly before you.*

PROVERBS 4:25

20

Speed Racer vs. Sunday Driver

---

*He drives fast and furious, zooming in and out
of traffic, while she putts along at fify miles
an hour in the center lane of the freeway.*

DID YOU EVER NOTICE that there's usually one person in a marriage who's Speed Racer behind the wheel, while the other is an aggravating Sunday driver—content to just putt-putt along at a snail's pace while they look at all the sights?

I'm the latter . . . and the former—depending on my mood or where I'm going and how late I am.

Consistency is not one of my strong suits. (Much to my husband's dismay.)

But I'm not the only one with schizo driving habits.

Our friend Mike O'Connor shared this great story with us about himself and his wife:

"Sally and I discovered something very interesting about each other when we first met," Mike said.

"When it came to our driving habits, I was overly cautious and she was semi-reckless. While our stands on other issues were more compatible, when we got seatbelted, I became William F. Buckley and she turned into the female Mario Andretti.

"This came out when I would need to make a left turn across heavy traffic at an intersection with no light, no left turn lane, or no suicide lane to cross one direction at a time.

"To me, the answer to this dilemma was obvious. Abdicate!

"Whenever this situation arose, I made an immediate right turn, then left on a subsequent street, did a U-turn in someone's driveway, and made a right turn down my intended street.

"I was now flowing with traffic the way God intended," Mike said.

151

"Proof of my victory came from seeing the car which had been waiting behind me—still stuck, trying to find a hole in traffic to shoot through."

This technique, however, drove Sally "stark, raving crazy."

"She spent a number of years going to school in Boston and New York where a driving test with only three pedestrians hit will net you a passing score," said Mike. "Her belief was that if you couldn't get across an intersection safely, you simply insinuate yourself into the oncoming traffic and hope that forces other cars to stop.

"I would point out that this was rude and selfish behavior," Mike said.

"She would point out that mine were cowardly and timid techniques." (She almost stopped dating him over this one issue.)

On a more reflective note, Mike says that it's interesting that years later they can look back and see that while Sally has become less reckless, he's started taking a few more chances—"not just in driving, but in many areas of our lives."

Then there's Robin and Scott.

Both are speed demons behind the wheel. Or at least, used to be, especially when Robin had her Corvette.

But that was before her baby was born—while she was still a cop.

She's now turned in the Corvette for a more sedate vehicle, and with baby in the car seat takes those country roads a lot slower these days.

Now, I've been known to put a little pedal to the metal when I'm in a hurry to get somewhere, too, but that's usually on the freeway when I'm all by myself. (Although my sister, Lisa, won't believe it when she reads that—the pedal to the metal part, that is.) Lisa's always giving me a hard time about my driving.

She says she pities the car behind me. She says I'm always taking my foot off the gas pedal—slowing down and speeding up. Slowing down and speeding up.

Constantly.

She accuses me of daydreaming and forgetting where I am—those times when I ease my foot off the pedal, never noticing cars passing by on the left *and* right sides of me.

But I don't know where she gets that idea. Just because she's known me more than forty years and has observed my daydreaming lapses up close and personal.

At least I've never had an accident.

Except for the time in high school when I rear-ended a school bus with my VW Bug.

But it wasn't my fault.

I'd glanced in my rearview mirror for just a second or two, when all of a sudden the big yellow bus in front of me stopped without warning.

And I plowed right into it—squashing my Bug and receiving a nice big scratch running from the top of my forehead down to the tip of my nose.

At least the cute boy in the car behind me rushed over to make sure I was okay. So it wasn't a total bust. (Although my parents didn't quite see it that way.)

Toni says that her husband, Les, refuses to let her drive anywhere.

"He says I'm too slow and dangerous for him. He says I don't pay attention and I talk on the phone too much.

"First of all, he's an aggressive driver," Toni says. "I don't care if we have nowhere to go or we have twenty minutes to get someplace that takes forty minutes. He has to weave in and out of traffic, never letting anyone get in front of him.

"I drive a bit differently," she said.

"And whenever—no matter how rare it is—I am driving and he's sitting on the passenger side, he has to be my mirrors: 'Watch out, honey, someone's coming over into your lane.... Did you see that car? ... Okay, you can get over now....'"

Toni says Les hates it when she's making a left turn because she starts off in one lane turning and ends up in the other lane by the time she completes her turn.

"Okay, that may be true," Toni admits. "But nobody is in either lane, so what difference does it make?

"Les also says I don't get over in the right lane soon enough when I want to get off the freeway. I think a quarter of a mile before the exit is good. He thinks it should be sooner—especially since I get mad when people won't let me over.

"And let's not talk about parking," Toni adds. "He's a madman about my driving around trying to get the closest parking spot. He will park three hundred miles away and walk.

"I don't want to do that.

"So I'll wait twenty minutes to get the close one. It takes him twenty minutes to walk from the spot he chooses, so what's the difference? My feet don't hurt by the time I get in the store, and I have more foot leverage to shop."

Although Toni's my dear friend and beloved sister in Christ, I'm afraid I'm going to have to side with Les on this one.

But that's probably because I'm kind of an impatient person.

I'd have to leap out of the car if I was trapped with Toni for twenty minutes while she drove around looking for that perfect spot. I just want to park the car, get in the store, buy what I need, and go on my merry way.

I don't have time to be cruising around parking lots all day.

Nor does Michael.

Thankfully, we're pretty alike in this area. However, we do have a major parking difference: what I call the "park-jerk response."

Michael will be driving through a parking lot looking for an empty space. He sees one and heads for it—turning his wheels in the direction of the space. Suddenly, at the last minute, he changes his mind and abruptly swerves or "jerks" the car around to park in a space in the opposite row.

That's when my entire body snaps forward and I wonder if suing my husband for whiplash is biblical.

We have a couple of driving differences too.

Take red lights.

Michael hates them, while I see them as an opportunity to catch up on my reading.

We'll be on our way to church or somewhere—usually running late—and Michael hits every red light.

He starts getting aggravated at the first one—convinced that it's a plot of the transportation and roads department to make him miss the next one too.

I tell him not to be so negative.

He tells me that it's a formula the way the lights are placed and timed, so that it's a sure thing if you hit the first red light, you're pretty well destined to hit every other one.

I never knew that.

Must be because a formula's involved.

I don't do formulas.

Blessed are they whose ways are blameless, who walk according to the law of the Lord.

PSALM 119:1

21

Fighting Habits of a Highly Ineffective Couple

How come no one gave us a fight instruction manual for a wedding gift?

"DON'T YELL AT ME," I pouted to my husband the first time he raised his voice to me.

He was amazed.

"You call this yelling?" he said. "You haven't *heard* yelling."

It's a tone thing for me.

To me, a raised voice is yelling. And I don't do yelling.

But to Michael, who with his actor's background can speak to a packed auditorium of 1,000 people without a microphone, a raised voice is simply projecting.

I just don't like it when it's projected onto me.

Everyone has a different fighting style.

Take our friends Bob and JoAnn Bryson.

JoAnn says she yells and screams and carries on, whereas Bob just clams up.

"It's like arguing with a rock," JoAnn said.

But she's figured out why: "He knows he's wrong, so he doesn't want to talk about it."

However, after forty-five years of marriage, they've learned how to resolve their differences—JoAnn goes shopping.

Then there's Dan and Karen Graham, married twenty-two years.

Karen tries to use reason and logic on Dan and it drives him nuts.

"He always said I should have been a trial attorney because I can take any subject and argue it any way—once I decide which way I want to win," Karen says.

She adds, however, that her logic isn't the typical black-and-white male logic that drives most of us women up the wall; it's more a manipulative lawyer-type logic.

"I think a woman doesn't feel like she's accomplished what she set out to do unless she wins him over to her way of thinking," says Karen. "If I don't win him over to my way of thinking, I've lost the fight."

Women hate to lose.

But more than that, we just want our husbands to admit they're wrong.

Recently one Sunday morning, our pastor, Ted Smith, was preaching on anger and he asked a question of the congregation. "If a man is walking alone in the woods talking to himself, and there's no woman there, is he still wrong?"

Michael roared with laughter until the tears came.

It's not so much that I want to win or have Michael admit that he's wrong; I just want him to *understand* where I'm coming from.

We'll be having an argument, and I'll be sharing my side, and sharing, and sharing, and sharing.

Until Michael finally says, "How much time are we going to spend on this?"

"I just want you to understand what I'm saying," I'll tell him.

"I do understand," he answers.

Then he repeats back to me what I've just said—in condensed male form using his I'm-in-a-hurry-no-non-sense tone of voice: "I said this. It made you feel like this. I won't say it again, and if I hurt your feelings, I'm sorry. Is that about it?"

Yes.

But he's lost all the feeling and emotions of the situation—which tells me he doesn't truly understand. He just wants to be done with the discussion so he can move on to more important things, like playing with his new scroll saw.

Then there's Toni and Les.

"Les doesn't know how to fight," says Toni. "I came from a family where you fight, you argue, you throw things. But he just says what he has to say and leaves the room.

"So I follow him and finish what I'm saying."

Toni tells Les that somebody needs to give him fighting lessons, because it's healthy to argue, and he doesn't even raise his voice.

Of course, if he ever does, Toni gets hurt and starts crying, "You hollered at me!"

I think a fight instruction manual would be a perfect wedding gift for new couples.

We got many useful gifts—from cookbooks to crock pots—but not one fighting instruction manual. And we could certainly have put it to good use.

The Grahams could probably find some use for such a manual too.

Karen says when they're arguing she'll keep pushing her husband's buttons until he reaches the point he calls "dumping the bucket load."

Then he starts to dump the bucket.

"He'll get louder and louder until he backs away and says, 'Well, you've done it now, I've got to go run,'" says Karen.

"I stay cool and calm and totally in control until he walks out the door, then once he's gone, I go in the bedroom and cry and have a pity party."

Karen says what she doesn't understand is that after a fight, most men are fine within ten minutes. They just blow it off and move on.

Not her.

"I'm like an elephant that never forgets," she says.

Dan will come back and say, "Oh hi, hon. Want to go for a cappuccino?" and Karen will say, "Don't you realize what just happened here ten minutes ago?"

"It's been closer to an hour," Dan says.

"I don't care," says Karen. "It's still on the same day and I can't just shrug it off."

I'm more of the shrug-it-off type person in our family—once I know Michael clearly understands my point of view.

Unless I'm really provoked. Then I may lose it and yell. (Although in our married history, I think I've only yelled twice. I'm just not a yeller.)

But Michael comes from a family of yellers. Even his brother, Pastor Bob, has been known to yell on occasion.

Family upbringing, more than gender, impacts the way people fight.

Take our Colorado pals Chuck and Lynn.

Chuck hates conflict. Lynn was raised on conflict.

In her family, lively debates and differences of opinion were the nightly norm at the dinner table. Therefore, an argument, to Lynn, is a way for them to grow closer.

Not Chuck.

"Conflict is candy to her and arsenic to me," he says.

Steve and Chris also have different fighting styles.

Although it wasn't until after they were married that Steve really saw Chris's Latin temper.

"When we were dating, I fought with Steve very calmly," says Chris. "Then after marriage, I had a raging fit—yelling and slamming doors. And Steve said to me, 'That will be the last time you slam a door.'"

"I couldn't believe someone said that to me," says Chris, admitting she was used to being a spoiled brat who had tizzy fits all the time. But she's learning now.

Then there's the couple who were having marital difficulties, and as a result, the husband had taken to sleeping on the couch.

His wife sought advice from her girlfriend on how to keep him in their bed.

"Pin his pillows to the bed," her friend said. "He'll get the feeling you want him to stay."

A fool gives full vent to his anger, but a wise man keeps himself under control.

PROVERBS 29:11

22

Keeping That Love Flame Burning

Grocery shopping together does not qualify as a date! How creative dating AFTER marriage helps keep that love flame burning brightly.

"MATE DATES" ARE an essential part of a happy marriage, say all the experts.

I agree.

But what exactly is a "date"?

For some, it's a romantic, candlelight dinner. For others, it's a picnic in the park.

And for still others, it's grocery shopping.

My friend Deirdre from Minnesota said she and her husband Jonathan like to go to Sam's Club—a discount grocery store that sells mass quantities to card-carrying members.

"We can spend hours there," Deirdre enthused. "We even hold hands."

"The ironic thing is that the day will probably never come when we'll need to buy twenty-four peach-colored washcloths at once or muffin mix in a box the size of a suitcase."

Of course, Deirdre and Jonathan are still newlyweds, so even going to the Laundromat is romantic to them. (Love that spin cycle.)

Some of us need a little more than that.

Our friends Chuck and Lynn, parents of three children, said they try for at least one weekend getaway a year on their anniversary "as it fits in around children being born, or nursing."

However, one bed-and-breakfast they went to had a bed that, in addition to sinking almost all the way to the floor, creaked quite loudly.

"The bedroom was right outside the kitchen where the bed-and-breakfast owner puttered around at night and early morning, so we didn't do all the activities we had planned," Lynn said with a smile.

Michael and I can relate to that.

Only it wasn't a creaky bed that stopped us.

Wanting to surprise me after a couple years of marriage, my sweet, thoughtful husband had booked two nights in a nice-sounding bed-and-breakfast in northern California.

He'd gotten the name and description of the place we'd be staying in from one of those two-for-the-price-of-one inn guides that you get when you send in cereal or tea box tops.

The first indication we had that perhaps the inn wouldn't be quite as delightful as it sounded, occurred when we spotted the neon sign boldly flashing the name of our charming bed-and-breakfast.

However, other than the tacky Las Vegas sign, the exterior of the building looked inviting, so we quickly quashed our neon-nervousness and walked inside.

As we checked in, we noticed a cardboard stand on the counter completely covered in bright red AIDS ribbons. Although it seemed a bit out of place in an establishment where one would usually expect to see leather-bound Shakespeare or the love poetry of Elizabeth Barrett Browning, we didn't think too much of it.

Until we were heading up to our room.

That's when Michael spotted a magazine on the coffee table boldly headlined "The Odysseus Guide to Gay Resorts."

Oops.

That was just the beginning of our very nonromantic anniversary weekend.

Now, Michael and I both love the whole atmosphere of old-fashioned bed-and-breakfasts: beautiful antiques, flowered wallpaper, crown molding, hand-stitched quilts, and claw-foot bathtubs.

So when our host proudly opened the door to our room, we got loads of atompshere—just not the kind we were expecting. (Somehow, the decorating gene had bypassed both innkeepers.)

Granted, there was a lovely antique oak double bed in the room, but it was covered with a garish black polyester bedspread dotted with hot pink tropical flowers.

The window coverings weren't quite as obnoxious—they were a soft, delicate rose pattern that looked remarkably like some bedsheets we had at home. In fact, as we got closer, we realized that they were, in fact, the missing pillowcases to our sheets!

And clearly they were hung up in a big hurry, too, because they were unevenly tacked to the window frame with a row of brightly-colored, mismatched thumbtacks.

Additionally, the taste-challenged decorator hadn't even bothered to slit open the seams on either side of the pillowcase to at least give the illusion of a curtain. (We briefly considered stuffing the curtains with our pillows for fun, but then thought better of it.)

And for the privilege of staying in this classy, romantic hideaway, we were paying nearly $100 a night. (Actually, with our two-for-one coupon, it was only $90 for both nights—such a deal!)

For some reason, neither of us felt too romantically inclined in this off-the-wall atmopshere, so it was a good thing Michael had packed his portable cribbage game.

We played seventeen rounds that night.

My poor husband. He felt terrible that his amorous plans had backfired so miserably.

But I told him not to worry about it—we'd just make the best of it. (If nothing else, it had great story value for later.)

Determined to salvage what we could of our romantic getaway, the next day we set off in our car to explore the area and look for some of the "quaint" antique shops our bed-and-breakfast guide had promised.

As we drove through town, though, we noticed that the streets were packed with wall-to-wall spandex-clad and body-pierced residents everywhere we looked.

We felt as if we'd beamed down to another planet. (And we really wanted Scotty to beam us back up, but he was nowhere to be found.)

At last we spotted a lovely-looking antique shop and went in, hoping to find one or two pieces of English bone china we might be able to afford.

Instead, we were greeted by vintage Gloria Swanson, Tallulah Bankhead, and Marilyn Monroe memorabilia.

Not exactly the antiques we were seeking.

When we finally got back home, we found out from some of our more well-traveled friends that the area we'd visited is renowned for its alternative lifestyles.

Just call us clueless. (We don't get out much.)

Oh well, that's one anniversary we won't soon forget.

Their one-month anniversary is one that Deirdre and Jonathan Thompson will always remember.

Deirdre surprised Jonathan by rushing home from work before him and setting up a tent in their living room. ("Not a challenge," she said, "since the only furniture we had were wedding gifts: two lawn chairs and two TV trays.")

She also sprinkled rose petals from the door of the apartment to the door of the tent where she waited with a supper of Diet Coke, crackers and cheese, and the remote control for a movie.

Now that's what I call creative dating.

My friend Annie Jornlin has been known to be a little creative—as well as sneaky—in dates with her husband, Bill.

One time she made Bill think they were going spelunking (cave exploring). "I told him to bring a rope, lantern, and coveralls," Annie said. Then she circled Cave City on a map and casually left it out where he would be sure to find it.

But instead of winding up deep down in a cave, Bill found himself on a riverboat for a romantic dinner cruise with his beloved.

Annie's a woman after my own heart.

Forget that dark, dirty, cold, claustrophobic cave

stuff, where you're apt to run into bats and mice and other creepy, crawly things!

Instead, give me a dinner cruise any day of the week. Michael, of course, would prefer Disneyland.

As would our friends Quenten and Doris.

In fact, Doris said to keep the "kid" alive in them and truly escape to Fantasyland, they spent four days at Disneyland for their twenty-fifth anniversary and had a ball. (They should have taken Michael, though, because that's probably the only way he'll ever make it to Disneyland on an annversary.)

Mickey and Donald just don't conjure up very romantic notions in my head.

Although . . . Michael might be able to persuade me if he threw in some Beauty and the Beast bubble bath, Godiva chocolates, and a night or two at the Hyatt.

I must admit, though, that I felt a little convicted about my selfish attitude when I heard what my friend Lisa's husband did for her.

Hank and Lisa have been married eighteen years, and like many men, Hank likes his football. But he likes his wife more. In fact, he's so in love with his bride that he gave up Monday Night Football to spend time with her instead.

Now instead of cheering for touchdowns, he makes a play for his wife on their standing Monday night date. (That man really knows how to score some points—and how to keep that love flame burning!)

> *"Many waters cannot quench love; rivers cannot wash it away."*
>
> SONG OF SONGS 8:7

23

Love Handles for the Romantically Impaired

Helpful hints for that romantically impaired man or woman in your life.

WHEN PEOPLE HEARD I was writing a book for the romantically impaired, they asked if I was planning to include specific suggestions for how their husbands and boyfriends (or wives and girlfriends) could be more romantic.

Luckily, there are already plenty of how-to books out there, but this isn't one of them.

That's why, in the spirit of fun and lightening up a little, I've developed a couple of foolproof "scientific" lists for that romantically impaired love of your life.

But before you give your beloved his or her list, you might want to go over the fine points on *yours* first.

Top Five Hints for the Romantically Impaired Man

5. Camping out is not a romantic getaway, but the Hyatt is.

4. W[h]ining and dining does not mean complaining about work while eating.

3. Going through the drive-thru with your low beams on doesn't count as a romantic candlelight dinner.

2. Forget that goofy saying, "Love means never having to say you're sorry." Apologize now, figure it out later.

1. Put the seat down!

Top Five Hints for
the Romantically Impaired Woman

5. The Hyatt is not a romantic getaway, but camping is.
4. Being on time means never saying, "I'm ready," and then not really being ready for another fifteen minutes.
3. Shopping is not a sports activity.
2. Whispering sweet nothings into his ear doesn't mean nagging.
1. A to-do list is not a love letter!

And we know that in all things God works for the good of those who love him.

ROMANS 8:28

For information on having Laura Jensen Walker speak at your event, please contact Speak Up Speaker Services toll free at (888) 870-7719 or e-mail Speakupinc@aol.com. To learn more about Laura, please visit her web site at www.laurajensenwalker.com. To write Laura, please e-mail her at Ljenwalk@aol.com or write to her at P.O. Box 601325, Sacramento, CA 95860.